D1303347

The Five Flirting Styles

Use the Science of Flirting to Attract the Love You Really Want

JEFFREY A. HALL, Ph.D.

 **HARLEQUIN**®

The Five Flirting Styles

ISBN-13: 978-0-373-89273-0

© 2013 by Jeffrey A. Hall

All rights reserved. The reproduction, transmission or utilization of this work in whole or in part in any form by any electronic, mechanical or other means, now known or hereafter invented, including xerography, photocopying and recording, or in any information storage or retrieval system, is forbidden without the written permission of the publisher. For permission please contact Harlequin Enterprises Limited, 225 Duncan Mill Road, Don Mills, Ontario, Canada, M3B 3K9.

Library of Congress Cataloging-in-Publication Data

Hall, Jeffrey A.

The five flirting styles : use the science of flirting to attract the love you really want / Jeffrey A. Hall, Ph.D.

pages cm
Includes bibliographical references and index.

ISBN 978-0-373-89273-0

1. Flirting. 2. Interpersonal relations. 3. Man-woman relationships.
I. Title.
HQ801.H3137 2013
306.73—dc23
2013002881

® and TM are trademarks owned and used by the trademark owner and/or its licensee. Trademarks indicated with ® are registered in the United States Patent and Trademark Office, the Canadian Trade Marks Office and/or other countries.

www.Harlequin.com

Printed in U.S.A.

CONTENTS

Introduction

A MISSED OPPORTUNITY

After a tough week of work, Kelsey was getting ready for a night on the town. Enjoying a preparty drink with her friends and blasting her favorite music, Kelsey took her time getting ready—she wanted to look good tonight. The kind of girl who brings the party wherever she goes, Kelsey seemed to know how to make friends with everyone. Bouncers, bartenders and waiters always wanted to give Kelsey—and her friends—a little something extra: a free drink, a good table, an extra appetizer. That night she was going to her favorite bar. She walked in and strutted up to the bar to get drinks for her friends. Although the bar was packed, Kelsey had no trouble getting the bartender's attention. As she flashed him a bright smile, the bartender came over to take her drink order. She leaned in to talk in his ear, and soon they were hitting it off like old friends. This was going to be a good night.

The same night, Spencer was getting ready to go out with his friends. For the first time in months, they had convinced him to try to meet someone—or so they thought. Spencer hated bars, clubs, basically the whole singles' scene. Despite what everyone said, he never found it a good way to meet women. He always ended up in a corner with an annoyed look on his face, watching other guys aggressively (and successfully) hit on girls. All his female friends told him how much they hate pushy guys, but once they were actually at the bar, the ladies seemed to love it. Despite what his friends thought, they hadn't convinced Spencer to finally get out and meet someone new. There was only one reason that he was going out—to see Kelsey.

He had met Kelsey at work. They were assigned to a new project that required long hours together. Gradually, over the weeks of working together, he thought there might be something between them. When he first met Kelsey, she was in a relationship (or something—she said it was complicated) with Justin. But, the last time Spencer saw her, she had confided in him that the relationship was over. Justin wasn't interested in anything serious. Every so often, Spencer got the impression that Kelsey might be interested in him. She was always going out of her way to talk to him and confide in him. When Spencer learned that Kelsey was going out with her friends, he let his friends know that he was finally up for a night out.

Meanwhile, Kelsey was having a great night. The bartender comped her first drink, and she was already feeling better about breaking up with Justin. After finishing her first round with her friends, she walked back up to the bar for round two. Almost immediately, a cute guy came over to her and bought her another drink. Kelsey loved it when guys hit on her. She knew it rarely went anywhere, but she didn't care. It was fun. Unfortunately, this new guy at the bar—what was his name again?—was boring, so it was time to find a way out. Thankfully, her escape walked through the door.

She knew Spencer from work, and she thought he was a really nice guy. He was always so friendly with her, and he was really a darling when she told him about that jerk Justin. While he was always sweet, she was pretty sure he wasn't into her. If he was, he certainly never let on or hit on her—at least not in a way she was used to. As Spencer walked in the door, she looked over the other guy's shoulder to smile at Spencer. Then, she beckoned Spencer over with her eyes the way she usually did with guys. But he didn't come up to the bar; he went straight to an empty booth with his friends. Kelsey thought, *What's his problem?*

I don't get it. Why is Kelsey talking to that guy? Spencer thought. *I swear she smiled at me when I walked in, but now she's hitting on someone else. I'm not going to compete with that.* He settled down at a booth with his friends and joined the conversation, trying not to let his disappointment show.

My drink's gone, and this guy is a tool. I'm going to go see what Spencer is doing, Kelsey thought. She found him in a booth with his friends. She came up behind him and playfully asked, "Hey, Spence! Planning to ignore me again?" Spencer turned, looking startled and a little embarrassed. But he moved over right away to make room for her beside him and he introduced her to his friends. Recognizing Spencer's interest, his friends walked to the bar to get another round of beers, leaving Spencer and Kelsey alone.

Spencer knew this was his chance. So he started talking to Kelsey. He asked her about Justin and if she was OK. He asked her about work and what she had been up to. He was exceedingly polite, but frustrated, too. Kelsey seemed to be a little bored and kept looking around the bar as if this weren't the place for having that sort of conversation. She looked amazing, but he thought better of saying so—he didn't want to come off as just another jerk. As the conversation wore down, she said, "I need to check in with my friends over there," nodding to the other section of the bar. Kelsey got up and said, "It was good to see you, Spence." Spencer was seriously disappointed, but he let her go and watched sadly as she walked away.

The story of Kelsey and Spencer happens over and over again, time after time, from California to Kansas, from Miami to Montreal. Girl wants to meet good guy, good guy wants to be with girl, but they just can't seem to connect. Kelsey's friends will later give her a hard time about always ending up with jerks like Justin, but can offer little advice about how to meet someone better. Spencer's friends will pick on him about how weak his game is and what a downer he is about going out, but they really can't offer any better advice.

Dating guides and pickup books won't help much, either. If you read these books, they'll tell you that Kelsey is a *good* flirt and Spencer is a *bad* flirt. But is Kelsey really a good flirt? Sure, Kelsey knows how to use her body language and bubbly personality to meet guys, but she always winds up with the wrong one. For Spencer, the dating guides will tell him, "Step up your game!" They'll tell him to get out there and compete with other men, to get her alone and come on strong because girls love a guy with confidence. As if it were as simple as that. Dating guides often tell women how to flirt with body language, as if batting your eyes or walking seductively is useful advice for everyone (or anyone).

FIVE FLIRTING STYLES

This book isn't like the others. This book is a game changer. The truth is there isn't just one *right* way to flirt. In fact, there are five flirting styles. You already have a way of flirting that feels natural and is most effective for you: you just need to learn how to use it. Rather than a one-size-fits-all approach, this book will give you detailed and research-based information about your own unique style of flirting so that you can flirt smarter and attract the kind of dates and relationships you really want to attract. That's what sets this book apart from the rest.

Based on exclusive research, these five flirting styles were discovered in a sample of over 5,000 eHarmony users and confirmed in a survey of 4,500 individuals worldwide. You will probably recognize yourself in one or more of these flirting styles. Everyone is a mix of the five styles, but typically one style is more dominant than the others.

- **The Physical Flirt:** Physical flirting involves the expression of sexual interest through body language. People who scored high in this style of flirting often develop relationships quickly and have more sexual chemistry with their partners.

- **The Polite Flirt:** The Polite style of flirting focuses on proper manners and nonsexual communication. Polite flirts like Spencer are less likely to come on to a potential partner and generally do not find direct flirting flattering, but they tend to have longer, more meaningful romantic relationships.

- **The Playful Flirt:** People with Playful flirting styles often flirt with little interest in romance. They flirt to have fun and for an ego boost, often with no romantic strings attached. Kelsey is a classic Playful flirt.

- **The Sincere Flirt:** Sincere flirting involves creating an intense emotional connection and communicating sincere interest. Sincere flirts have meaningful romantic relationships that put emotional connection first and sexual attraction second.

- **The Traditional Flirt:** Traditional flirts believe men should make the first move and women should not pursue men. By taking a more passive role in dating, Traditional women have trouble getting men's attention and are less likely to be direct in expressing their intentions. Likewise, Traditional men often know a potential partner for a longer time before approaching her.

Your style of flirting isn't inherently good or bad. But understanding your flirting style—and how to recognize all five flirting styles—can be invaluable in your dating life. That's because how you flirt influences the way you communicate attraction, the kind of person you attract, your relationship success and how long a relationship you typically have. If you're not finding the kind of relationships you want, your flirting style isn't working for you—and that's where this book can help.

In the following chapters, you will find out how your flirting style influences your love life and read all about the real experiences of people just like you. You will discover what kind of messages you are sending when you flirt—are you giving off signs that you're interested in a quick fling or a serious relationship? You will also learn the best places to find love, based on your flirting style. (Turns out Polite flirts like Spencer are better off avoiding the bar scene altogether in their search for love.) And by learning about all five flirting styles, you'll be able to identify them when you see them in other people. You'll avoid missed opportunities, like the one described above involving Kelsey and Spencer, by recognizing when someone is genuinely interested. And when you can figure out your newest crush's style of flirting, you'll know more about how they say, "I like you" and whether they are likely to ever say, "I love you." Armed with a little self-reflection and better insight into the actions and motivations of others, you'll have a serious advantage in the singles scene. Most importantly, you will learn how to make your flirting style work for you.

TAKE THE FLIRTING STYLES INVENTORY

Just how will you find out your own flirting style? Take the online Flirting Styles Inventory (http://flirtingstyles.dept.ku.edu/). The questions on the Flirting Styles Inventory were selected based on my analysis of data from 5,000 eHarmony daters. The online

Flirting Styles Inventory was developed to give people clear and research-based feedback on their own flirting style in relation to people their same age and sex. This online survey will give you individualized feedback about how *you* flirt, not how you *should* flirt.

When the online Flirting Styles Inventory was first introduced, it went viral. Almost 60,000 people all over the world took my Flirting Styles Inventory to learn about their own style of communicating attraction. Bonnie Rochman, who blogged about the five flirting styles for *Time* magazine on Valentine's Day, encouraged her readers to take the inventory to find out "if the survey results capture your personality as accurately as they did mine." The online Flirting Styles Inventory will provide you with a personalized perspective about your own approach to initiating romance.

The new and improved Flirting Styles Inventory (FSI) will compare your particular flirting style against the 5,000 original eHarmony users and interviews with over 4,500 daters throughout the world. The personal experiences of nearly 10,000 people of all ages and demographics (single, married, divorced, male and female) will help you learn about your own flirting style. The FSI is designed to tailor the feedback to your age and gender. This means that if you are a 24-year-old woman, your flirting style will be compared to women 21-25 who have taken the inventory, rather than, say, 35-year-old men. This sort of detail will give you a perspective that you simply cannot get anywhere else. Beyond this one-of-a-kind feedback from the online FSI, the information in this book will change your perspective on your own flirting style by sharing the collective perspective of thousands of daters.

FLIRTING STYLES AND DATING SUCCESS

This book includes the best research on flirting styles you'll find anywhere. In fact, it is the only book on flirting styles you'll find. You will learn about how Kelsey's Playful style of flirting typically results in short-term relationships. You will learn that the typical Kelseys of this world, while seen by friends as excellent flirts, may not always get the kind of relationship they want. The Playful style of flirting makes some things more likely to happen, like getting a free drink, but other things less likely to happen, like attracting a man who wants a long-term relationship. More importantly, most of the Kelseys out there don't even realize how their flirting style influences their dating life.

You will learn about how Polite flirts like Spencer often take a long time to make the first move. You will learn why Polite flirts often hate the singles scene, and why, if they are men, they are more likely to have friends who are girls than girlfriends. Although Polite flirts believe they are flirting by asking questions and being respectful, oftentimes their crush just doesn't get it. This book will give Polite flirts a variety of effective suggestions and strategies to get that message across in a way that matches their own distinctive way of communicating interest.

In the following pages you will also find out why, despite what you might read in other books, Kelsey isn't necessarily a *better* flirt than Spencer. Depending on whether you want a short- or long-term relationship, whether you prefer a slow- or fast-paced courtship, whether you want to connect sexually or emotionally, one flirting style may be better for you than another. People have different goals and motivations for flirting, and each flirting style is more or less effective at achieving each of those goals.

With this book, you will get tailored advice about how to be a more effective flirt and attract the type of person you really want to attract. Learning about your particular style will enable you to convey your attraction and intentions more effectively, so you can achieve your particular relationship goals. You might be a terrible flirt in one situation and a great one in another. Learning about yourself and what you want to achieve will help you reach your goals.

This book might not make you an instant flirting success, but it will help you take the first steps toward a journey of making your flirting style work for you.

HOW TO USE THIS BOOK

First, go online and complete the online Flirting Styles Inventory (http://fiveflirtingstyles.dept.ku/edu/). You will get your own individualized report that you can download, print and share (if you like). Once you know your flirting style, this book will explain how your style influences every step of a relationship—from where you go to meet people to how you experience love in committed relationships. You can zero in on the chapters and sections that focus on your own flirting style, but don't skip the parts about the other flirting styles. Flirting takes two, after all, so you'll want to know how *other* people flirt, too.

Here is a quick summary of what's to come in the rest of *The Five Flirting Styles.* In Chapter 1, "The Five Flirting Styles," you will learn more about how the five flirting styles came to be. You'll learn how the Physical, Polite, Playful, Sincere, and Traditional styles were discovered, and how the Flirting Styles Inventory was created, bringing together the collective experiences of over 5,000 eHarmony daters. You'll also learn about the three pathways to romance: the Hookup, the Known Quantity and the First Date. Depending on your flirting style, one of these pathways may be a better way to find romance than another.

The next five chapters offer detailed information about each flirting style. After getting a rundown of the personality and characteristics of people with each flirting style, you'll find out about notable differences between men and women in all five styles. You'll learn about how different flirts seek out romance in different places, and what happens once they go on that first date. You'll find answers to questions like, Where do people with your flirting style go to meet new flings and find serious relationships? That way you'll know where to go to meet people compatible with your flirting style. Each chapter will also tell you about flirting styles in the bedroom. What can your flirting style say about your sex life? Quite a lot, it turns out. You'll also discover how your flirting style matters for long-term commitment and love. When people flirt, they are at the very first stages of falling in love. How you flirt influences how fast or slow you take those first steps toward romance.

Chapter 7 is all about "The Switch." The switch is an internal on or off button that fundamentally changes our communication and perception of attraction. You will learn in this chapter what being on and being off feels like, and get some key insights into how you can tell where you stand. You'll learn how to get a better grasp of your own switch, and learn some techniques for turning your switch on *and* off. Becoming adept at adjusting your internal switch will make all the difference in helping you learn how to use your flirting style to communicate attraction and understand when others are flirting with you.

Everyone wants to know the answer to the question, How can I tell if someone is flirting with me? In Chapter 8, "Perceptions and Misperceptions," you'll get the answer to that question broken down into nine simple rules. You'll find out the differences between men and women in the way they communicate attraction and what sorts of mistakes in perceiving attraction each makes. Using the best and most up-to-date research on attraction, I'll tell you what nonverbal behaviors to look for to determine if someone is flirting, and what you can do to clarify the message you send out to others.

Finally, Chapter 9, "Common Mistakes and Helpful Hints," will offer you practical and tailored advice about flirting. People often find themselves frustrated or unhappy because they can't seem to get others to notice them, to find them interesting, and to know they are interested in romance, not friendship or just a short-term hookup. This chapter will help you learn about the types of mistakes that are common to your own flirting style. By knowing more about your own flirting mistakes (and those of other people very much like you), you gain insight into why you might end up where you do and how you might change. This chapter will offer some helpful hints about how to make your flirting style work for you. While Chapter 9 is dedicated to this useful information, this invaluable advice is by no means in only one chapter. In every single chapter there is clear and helpful advice specific to your flirting style.

Chapter One

THE FIVE FLIRTING STYLES

The book you're reading began with an incredibly lucky meeting of minds in Los Angeles, which evolved into an academic research article and then sparked a viral media explosion. The five flirting styles have received incredible media coverage on TV, in print and online. *Cosmo, Glamour, USA TODAY* and *Time* magazine, among many others, featured my five flirting styles. In this chapter, I'll explain the research and exclusive data behind the five flirting styles. I'll also give you a crash course in the true definition of flirting (which is much more than "batting eyes") and how we go about communicating attraction, setting the stage for how the flirting styles came to be and how this approach is fundamentally different than what came before.

HOW IT ALL GOT STARTED

RESEARCH SAYS

For years, school, work, and through friends and family were the most common places to meet a new spouse. Internet dating is now second only to meeting through friends.

The story of the five flirting styles starts with a seismic shift in dating as we know it, as online dating became more and more popular. After years of slow, steady growth in the 1990s, online dating services experienced exponential growth between 2000 and 2005. This posed a special challenge for matchmaking services that pair members with other members based on key data they collect. This was the challenge that the senior director for research and product development at eHarmony, Steve Carter, was charged with addressing.

In order to better serve eHarmony users and ensure a higher success rate—a better match, if you will—Steve wanted research on the science of romantic chemistry. When two people were matched by eHarmony, courted through email and were confident enough to meet face-to-face, what happened? Did they experience that electric spark of chemistry or was it dullsville? Steve wanted data about eHarmony users that would help sort out the matches who felt a strong connection as opposed to those who felt nothing.

At that time I was an eager new graduate student at the Annenberg School for Communication at the University of

Southern California. My advisor, Dr. Michael Cody (Cody to his friends), had a friend and former student named Julie Albright who knew Steve Carter, who was a USC psychology grad. At that time, Cody and I were writing a book chapter on pickup lines, and Julie passed along this info to Steve. At the Daily Grill in downtown Los Angeles, and later at eHarmony headquarters in Pasadena, I found myself at this fortuitous meeting of the minds.

QUOTABLE

"How a person flirts honestly reveals some important qualities about the individual."

—Dr. Steven Gangestad, evolutionary psychologist at the University of New Mexico

The one thing we all had in common was an interest in flirting. Cody had studied people's perception of whether someone is flirting with them or not. I was interested in learning whether pickup lines are *ever* effective (sometimes) and whether particularly good-looking guys can get away with saying obnoxious lines to women (yes, they can). Julie had her ear to the ground, researchwise, learning firsthand about dating from people on the singles scene. To help answer his questions, Steve offered us access to eHarmony members who wanted to participate in an online study on flirting. This was an amazing opportunity— eHarmony rarely opened up its doors to outside researchers. Yet, here I was, armed with access to thousands of active daters and a crack team with vast research experience. But what questions were we going to ask our volunteers? What did we want to know? Like a good graduate student, I did some research.

THE SURVEY SAYS

Most women claim to hate pickup lines, but nearly 70 percent of women agreed that a "cheesy line" delivered by the "right person" is inviting.

WHAT IS FLIRTING?

People think that there is just one way to flirt: through body language. But I came to the conclusion that pinning down flirting is a lot harder than you might think. I set off to try to answer these three questions.

1. Do you always know when someone is flirting with you?
2. Does everyone flirt for the same reason or with the same goal in mind?
3. Is the body language of a flirtatious person different than that of a friendly person?

After looking at the evidence, I had to come to these conclusions: *No!*, no and sort of (in that order). One of the big discoveries of the flirting styles project was this: Everyone simply does not flirt in the same way or for the same reasons.

Show it, know it?

What is flirting? It resembles the Supreme Court's famous definition of pornography—"I don't know, but I know it when I see it." Oddly enough, a lot of people don't fit this definition, either—they don't even know it when they see it. In addition to the well-known fact that men are happily overoptimistic (and wrong) in thinking a woman is flirting with them, nearly everyone in our survey said that they had been in a situation where someone was flirting with them and they didn't even know it.

The opposite problem also happens all the time. A woman, say, uses every move she knows to try to give someone the hint that she is interested, but without success. It seems that most people would not know if a behavior constituted flirting, even if they saw it (or sometimes even if it hit them over the head). One study concluded that flirting is harder to read than friendliness, anger and rejection! It seems that people flirt so differently, it is hard to know it if you see it.

THE SURVEY SAYS

Almost all of us (90 percent) have been in the situation where someone else thought we were flirting, but we weren't meaning to.

What's your MO?

Another challenge in figuring out what is flirting and what isn't is that people have very different goals when they're flirting. I am often asked the same question in many different forms:

"How do you know if someone is really flirting with you or is just being nice/trying to get a free drink/trying to make someone else jealous?" The problem is, you really can't tell. People will often do things that look like flirting for reasons that have nothing to do with love, romance or attraction. Because of the utterly contradictory and confusing goals that people can have and the unfortunate possibility of outright deception when flirting, it is hard to know whether or why someone is flirting at all.

THE SURVEY SAYS

Almost all of us (91 percent) have been in the situation where we thought someone was flirting with us, but we were wrong.

Look for the Signs

Another popular way of thinking about flirting is to look for the nonverbal signs: a sweet smile; a light touch on the hand; deep eye contact; quickly touching or fixing hair; a shy, covert look; and a confident strut across a crowded room. The problem with this approach isn't that it isn't accurate—all of those behaviors *are* flirting. The problem is that there are lots of things going on when two people are trying to make a connection. We want to make a good impression, so we are really focused on ourselves and planning what to say. It is hard to decipher what the actions of other people mean when we are so worried about making a good impression.

What is flirting?

We decided that flirting occurs when one person expresses sexual or romantic interest in another person, is the target of such an expression or is engaged with another person in just trying to figure out if the feeling is mutual. If you are trying to flirt—no matter how successful you are—then you are flirting. If a man is flirting with you—whether you pick up on it or not—then he is flirting. If you are just talking to someone new and in the process realize that you like him and think he likes you back—then you are flirting. Flirting is the communication and discovery of romantic or sexual interest. And, as the research shows, there are different ways to do so.

One Size Does Not Fit All

Think about it. If everyone behaved the same, then flirting would be easy: just bat eyes twice, smile sweetly three times, laugh coyly, then ta-da: flirting. The one-size-fits-all approach to flirting says there is just one way to do it and you are either good or bad at it. But people have different approaches and different goals when flirting and dating. Flirting is challenging enough as it is, because all of us flirt in our own way and for our own reasons. The flirting styles approach helps to clarify why you flirt the way you do by taking into account all the richness and complication in the dating world and reducing it to five intuitive styles of flirting. I believe there are many paths to the same goal, and this book will let you know just how well your style fits your particular path.

DIFFERENT PATHS
TO THE SAME GOAL

Have you ever met someone and felt love at first sight? This is the wonderful feeling that washes over you when you meet someone for the first time and you just *know* that this person is for you. If you haven't felt that way before, you might be somewhat disappointed or envious of people who have experienced it. Let's consider something different: Have you ever fallen in love with a friend? Maybe for you, going through the experience of getting to know someone, seeing him first as a confidante, a friend or a coworker made you see him in a new light. By knowing him for a while, you saw that he was a wonderful and special person. You couldn't help but desperately *want* to become closer to him, and you enjoyed each step on this path of discovery. If you never had this experience, you might sigh, and say, "How romantic!" Then, there is one last possibility: Have you ever gone out on a date with someone, really getting to know him for the first time, and it was perfect? You barely knew him before, but you didn't want the night to end?

The truth is, all three of these paths exist. The first seems pretty well-suited to flirting, but the second, not so much. If flirting happened only at a club, a bar or a party—places where chemistry and attraction are in bloom—then love at first sight would be the only way to find love. But love doesn't always happen at first sight. In fact, there are three distinct paths to romance. Each is a legitimate and meaningful way to go about falling for someone. And each is better suited to a different style of flirting.

QUOTABLE

"How people initiate relationships is important. It could be linked to the ultimate quality of relationships."

—Paul Eastwick, assistant professor, University of Austin, Department of Human Development and Family Sciences

The Hookup

Of the three pathways to romance, the hookup is the one that people probably think about most often when they picture flirting. This is a path of passion and chemistry, rather than discovery and slow romance. "I want to get to know you" is less important than "I want you." You have been on this path if you have ever hooked up with someone at a bar or at a party, if you ever joined the party in Cancun on spring break, or if you ever started a serious relationship after what you thought was a one-night stand or a quick fling. Hooking up could just be a kiss or a little making out, but it is also the pathway to the booty call and the one-night stand. It is love at first sight and head over heels types of romance. The one thing that ties all these things together is the tight bond among physical attraction, romantic attraction and sexual attraction.

WHO DOES THIS?

Although there are no studies that look at the rates of hooking up for all Americans, there is good evidence that young adults and college students hook up *a lot*. Elizabeth Paul and her colleagues found that about 80 percent of college students hook up at some point in college. On average, they do it about once a month. Another way of looking at it is to find out what sort of action people are getting, then find out where they are getting it. In one study of young adults, the majority were sexually involved with a steady boyfriend or girlfriend. For that group, sex always took place in the context of a committed relationship. However, the second most common type of sexual activity was found among young adults who played the field regularly. Both of these studies found that hooking up was a pretty common pathway to sexual activity.

LOVE AT FIRST SIGHT

Another way to think about the hookup as a pathway to a romantic relationship is to think about whether or not people know they are romantically interested right away. Dick Barelds and Pieternel Barelds-Dijkstra, a pair of Dutch researchers, got a representative sample of people involved in relationships, and asked them how they got there. About 40 percent of them reported that their relationship grew from love at first sight. These lovers seek out passionate love affairs and quickly move into relationships.

The First Date

The second pathway to romance is the first date. We all know what a first date is. In a nutshell, two people go out together to get to know each other better. The first date pathway includes every relationship that got started by people who barely knew each other at first, and went out on a date to get to know each other better. This would be like asking someone who works out at your gym to go out with you. This would certainly include any-one who goes out on a date after being matched up or initiating contact through an online dating site. This absolutely includes the blind date. It also includes the classic and formal, "I would like to take you out sometime" date where you go to dinner and a movie with the barista from the local coffee shop.

WHO DOES THIS?

The same researchers who looked at love at first sight also looked at people whose pathway to a relationship was from acquaintance to dating to love. These people did not know they were in love right away, but went out a few times to see if there was any potential. Although this was less common than the hookup pathway, about 35 percent of people started down the first date path to romance.

The first date pathway is more common among people whose personal and private life is detached from their daily working life. This is simply not the case for most college students. For them, the line between hanging out and going on a date is extraordi-narily blurry. College students spend time with potential boy-friends and girlfriends where they live, when they hang out, while they attend classes with one another and any time they go to a party. This means there is no beginning and no end of a "date" (if it should even be called that). It is *all* hanging out. For most adults, it's not as if you can kick off from work in the middle of the day to hang out without purpose or time limitations with your newest crush. (Maybe you could if both of you don't have jobs. But then you have another problem on your hands.)

The first date path is also distinct from the hookup because each of you knows why you are there: you are on a date. This means you dress up, look good, spend time alone and ask personal questions. Looking good is also part of the hookup experience, but time alone and personal questions? Nope and nope. When people go on dates, the most common reason is to figure out whether they want to develop something more. And the better you know someone, the more likely it is that the date actually *means* something. When people who are more than casual acquaintances go on a date, they are there to escalate the relationship to a new level.

This move to go on a date with someone you already know is what I like to call a *context shift*. By shifting context, from busy work life to a private table at a restaurant, from online chatting to a face-to-face meeting, you shift the nature of the relationship. These context shifts play a key role in defining your relationship and how it develops (or doesn't). They frame expectations and tell the people who are on that date what to expect.

The Known Quantity

The last path is the friends-first relationship type. What's particularly interesting about this path is that it's rarely mentioned in magazines or dating guides. People think of dates. People think of hookups. People almost never think about the slow process of becoming close emotionally or becoming companions and then starting a relationship. Barelds and Barelds-Dijkstra estimate that about 25 percent of people started out their relationship as friends first. It might be the minority of the three pathways, but not by much.

Some people like to get to know a person before ever making themselves available romantically. Part of the reason for this is that these people take love very seriously. They are looking for a romantic partner who suits them, who shares their values and interests, and who has long-term potential. They are looking for someone they can share a life with.

But this pathway doesn't just include long-term friends, like the classic friends-turned-lovers story of *When Harry Met Sally*. This pathway includes people who get together after knowing each other for a long time through work, school or a house of worship. These are people who never really considered each other as relationship potential, not because they weren't attractive, but because they didn't make themselves available or weren't available when they first met. The known quantity path is about getting to know someone for a long time before engaging them romantically.

RESEARCH SAYS

No matter what your pathway to romance, all end up in equally satisfying relationships.

HOME TURF

There are two reasons I am going into detail about these three pathways. First, this gives us more evidence that there is not just one way to start a relationship or to flirt with someone. More importantly, I want to make it clear that different flirting styles lead to different pathways to romance. Once you know your flirting style, you can get a better idea of where your particular style might shine. It is like having a home field advantage. You are more comfortable there and you know better what to expect. Rather than seeking love in a place totally unsuited to your style of flirting, if you get to know your own flirting style, you can look for romance in the best place you can be. Also, if you want to meet a person with a certain flirting style, you'll know where to go to find one. Knowing where a flirt finds love—or at least where he seeks it out—can tell you a lot about his style of flirting and what makes him so effective. You'll do a much better job speaking the same language as other attractive singles if you go to a place where your flirting style is welcome and acceptable, rather than off-putting and out of character (think of Polite Spencer in that bar).

WHY FIVE STYLES?

All of us who worked to develop the five flirting styles—the flirting styles team—were communication and social psychology researchers, so we knew that everyone is simply not the same. Some people are more assertive and others are more submissive. Some people are energetic and outgoing and others are quiet and introverted. People have different styles of communication. Knowing all this, we agreed that there was simply no way that everyone had the same flirting style.

To pinpoint the flirting styles we looked to flirting's close relative—communication. Fortunately, there is a significant body of research about people's various styles of communication. Communication researchers know that the *way* a message is communicated is central to understanding its meaning. Essentially, communication researchers were the first to claim, "It isn't what you said, it was the way you said it." Looking to the way that something is said or done tells you a lot about what that person means. Think of sarcasm. You can't just take a sarcastic person at face value—quite the opposite, in fact. Similarly, your style of flirting tells other people how to interpret your message, no matter what you are saying.

We All Have a Certain Style

The style of communication concept is particularly helpful when the things people say are ambiguous and when being direct is unwelcome or ineffective. This is exactly the situation when you are flirting. You are intentionally trying to be indirect but you are simultaneously looking for clues to clarify ambiguity in the other person. In fact, you might not even know if you are interested in the other person yet—maybe you are trying to figure that out. Or maybe, once you realize that Mike from the HR department isn't just being nice but is totally into you, Mike just got a lot more interesting. Whatever the situation, your particular style of communicating romantic interest will play a big role in how things turn out. What our research revealed was that how you flirt in the early stages of getting to know someone matters quite a bit in predicting the speed, success and selection of partners in romantic relationships. Our flirting style changes, influences and determines how we flirt, date and love!

THE SURVEY SAYS

Immediate sexual chemistry is less common than you think—less than half of people experience it with their new crush.

Backed by the research on communication styles, I set off to discover the primary styles of communicating romantic attraction. You can think of a flirting style as a particular manner of conveying interest in the opposite sex. Each style *on its own* could be a meaningful pathway to expressing attraction and starting a relationship. After reading lots of past studies on dating, courtship and flirting, I discovered that each of the five styles were right there in front of me—but no one had put them all together before.

A Little of This, a Little of That

Before telling you what I discovered, it is important to keep in mind that everyone employs all five styles to some extent. Most people score very high on one or two styles of flirting, very low on another and in the middle for the final two. While everyone is usually dominant in one or two styles, it is very unlikely that anyone scores at the top of one style and at the bottom of all of the rest. This means it is also unlikely that a person scores toward the bottom of every style. In reading about these five styles, keep in mind that everybody is a mix of each flirting style, scoring high or low on each. So if you are thinking, "I don't have a flirting style," just take the online Flirting Styles Inventory (the FSI for short) to find out where you stand, compared to others who are just like you. (See page xi on how to take the FSI online.)

THE PHYSICAL STYLE

The first style was the easiest to uncover because it is the one most of us think of when we think of flirting—if one style typifies the universal definition of flirting, the Physical style is it. People will say that if you want to know if a woman is flirting, look at her body language. Look at her hands, hips, eyes and smile. For most people (and for most academic researchers), observing what people do physically with their body, face and voice is the best way to know if they are flirting. Translating these behaviors into a style was relatively straightforward: the Physical flirt feels comfortable and confident using her body language to communicate interest. Physical flirts are not shy about letting a potential partner know how they feel and they do so through their physicality, nonverbal behavior and physical attractiveness. They know what they've got going for them and aren't afraid to use it.

THE SURVEY SAYS

Nearly 75 percent of women admit to trying to "casually bump into a guy" to get his attention.

A Physical flirt experiences the following things quite often: other people interpret his everyday manner as more sexually charged, he has little difficulty letting others know he is interested and he thinks other people are flirting with him everywhere he goes. On the opposite end of the spectrum, individuals low in the Physical style would be uncomfortable expressing their romantic interest in a physical or sexual way, and would be slow to show their interest in another person with their body language.

A Physical Style, Not Sex

To clear up a couple of points of confusion, the Physical flirting style does not directly tap into a person's sex life, sexuality or attitudes about sex. In Chapter 2, "The Physical Style," you'll get the lowdown on what the Physical flirting style says about a person's sex life. For now, it is important to keep in mind that having a Physical style isn't just about sex. We all know someone who is very touchy-feely. We know that this person enjoys and is comfortable with physical touch, but this doesn't mean that she is interested in having sex with everyone she hugs. The other thing is that the Physical style of flirting doesn't make you Don Juan. This is an important distinction between the flirting styles approach and other perspectives on flirting: your flirting style doesn't make you a "good" flirt. As we will see in future chapters, Physical flirts have more success doing certain things, but are less successful at others.

RESEARCH SAYS

Your physical attractiveness can change dramatically during a first date. Your personality affects how sexy other people perceive you to be. What you say can either enhance or undermine how physically attractive your date perceives you to be.

THE POLITE STYLE

The Polite flirt is a very careful flirt. He minds his Ps and Qs and good manners are a must. The Polite flirting style is a rule-governed and cautious approach to the communication of romantic interest. This style embraces politeness, refuses to engage in inappropriate or obviously sexual behavior, diligently follows courtship rules and adopts a cautious approach to relationship initiation. The Polite flirt is especially concerned about avoiding the image of looking needy, trying too hard, embarrassing himself, losing control or appearing too aggressive or insensitive. Although these are worries everyone has when flirting, the Polite flirt believes that following the rules is much more important than being direct.

What is particularly interesting about the Polite flirt is that she doesn't like it when someone else aggressively flirts with her. The Polite flirt feels that forward people are rude and (gasp!) impolite. As a consequence, she is slow-paced and quite indirect in her communication of attraction. Think of someone who is very intrigued by someone she just met, but rather than being assertive, playful or overtly pushy, she is careful, kind and cautious. This new potential partner may have no idea that the Polite flirt is flirting at all, but for the Polite flirt, this is the way it is done. Although the Polite flirt is rather inhibited in her way of communicating romance, that doesn't mean she doesn't want to develop physical chemistry or end up in bed eventually. What this means for the Polite flirt (and for those who are being hit on ever so politely by a Polite flirt) is that she is keeping her physical feelings in check for the sake of romance. To the Polite flirt, being out-and-out direct when engaging in romance is simply uncouth.

THE SURVEY SAYS

Nearly 60 percent of daters hate it when loud music gets in the way of good conversation.

Polite flirts have more conservative attitudes about dating and courtship. The Polite flirt feels uncomfortable meeting new people at parties or clubs, and is likely to prefer more low-key or genteel settings, like coffee shops or church. For this style, a nonsexual approach is preferred, and forward or direct advances by prospective partners are threatening or unwelcome. By contrast, those who score low on the Polite style behave in an incautious manner, worry less about social conventions, and, if need be, will use forward or aggressive tactics during courtship.

THE PLAYFUL STYLE

The Playful flirt sees flirting as a game. For the Playful flirt, it is fun to meet people, to chat them up, and to try to get other people to fall for them. The Playful style is bubbly, funny, flirty and fun. Playful flirts simply do not believe that you should flirt with someone only because you want to have some sort of relationship—either a hookup or a marriage. Playful flirts are just not worried how other people may interpret their behavior as long as they're having a good time. A flirtatious interaction is done for its own sake—no (romantic) ties required.

THE SURVEY SAYS

Playful flirts are the only flirting style to flirt even when they are not physically attracted to someone, and the only style to say, "I will flirt at every opportunity."

Boost That Self-Esteem

In the process of discovering the five flirting styles, I noticed an interesting trend in academic research. We began to document what flirting does for the communicator. On the top of that list: flirting makes you feel good. By attracting attention, being engaging and playing little games that come along with flirting, you feel sexy, exciting, inviting and desirable. It is simply a self-esteem boost. Notice that none of these things are even remotely about finding someone good enough for tonight, much less for a lifetime. The Playful flirt embraces all these added bonuses that come along with flirting and really doesn't care if it leads anywhere relationshipwise.

The bottom line: Flirting can be done for reasons other than starting a relationship. You might flirt to get a cop to let you out of a speeding ticket or flirt with a waitress at a restaurant or, if you work in retail, you might flirt with a shopper to get him to bring out the high-limit credit card. The Playful flirt knows this and has absolutely no problem with it.

Not for Very Long

What this means, though, is that actually getting into a long-term relationship is tricky for the Playful flirt. Not only does he have to put aside the endless temptations to flirt with other people, he has to follow through and try to keep one and only one person interested. This is a tough challenge for the Playful flirt. And, once in a relationship, just try to tell him not to flirt with other people. I have a friend who flirts with waitresses while out on a date with his *wife!* He is still married and even has a little girl, so that doesn't mean he isn't loyal. The two of them just had to accept that it is hard for him to turn off the charm when he sees a chance for a little shot of self-esteem.

THE SINCERE FLIRT

The Sincere flirt flirts by showing sincere and personal interest. This flirting style is marked by a desire to create an emotional bond with a new crush. The Sincere flirt knows that one of the primary ways to develop intimacy on a first date is to share things about yourself and get the other person talking, too. The Sincere flirt takes this old saying to heart: If you want to be an interesting person, get someone to talk about himself. The Sincere flirting style is defined as a desire to communicate romantic or sexual interest by paying sincere attention to a potential partner's underlying personality. The Sincere flirt conveys attraction by looking for an emotional connection, as opposed to sexual interest. She may also be sexually interested in another person, but for her, sexual chemistry evolves *through* communication and self-disclosure. Sexual chemistry may develop, but it takes a back seat to an emotional connection.

People Like It

This style of flirting is highly preferred and effective. Seeking an emotional connection with a partner is rated as the most agreeable, desirable and most honest of all strategies. No doubt this is likely why it is also the most common flirting style.

Wait a second. You may be wondering, If people know that showing interest, being sincere and asking questions are surefire ways to build intimacy and closeness, why doesn't everyone do it? Even if people know that something works, that doesn't mean they can do it naturally, confidently or effectively. Like the Physical style, people might know that a little physicality will up their chances of being noticed by the opposite sex, but it may not come easily to them. A Sincere style of flirting may be boring or slow-paced for someone who doesn't like all the *talking* it requires. Also, because it is generally nonthreatening and nonsexual, and some people like a little danger and fun in dating, the Sincere style could be a bad fit. Although the Sincere style is effective and very common, it just isn't everyone's thing.

THE TRADITIONAL STYLE

The Traditional style of flirting revolves around the idea that, in dating, men should make the first move and women should not pursue men. It may seem strange that, despite changes in our society, this style of flirting would still be around, but Traditional flirts still follow this pattern. In fact, they insist on it. For Traditional flirts, a strong belief in separate roles for men and women not only guides their own behavior, but it influences how they see other people. A very Traditional woman might say things like, "I expect a man to do all the work when we are dating" and "I expect a man to put me on a pedestal" and "I deserve to be treated like a lady." A very Traditional man might say, "Women who are too forward are probably promiscuous" or "Men who do not take the lead on a date are not real men." Clearly, the Traditional style is tied up in tightly defined rules and roles: men are men and women are women.

THE SURVEY SAYS

Nearly 25 percent of men said that they have had to work hard to get a woman interested. Only 9 percent of women said that they had to work hard to get a man interested.

Read from a Script

This style is important in figuring out who does what to whom on a date. As we all know, there is a well-defined series of events—or a script—that occurs during a date: Men ask women out. Men pick women up. Men open doors for women. Men pick up the tab at dinner, and so on. There is also a well-defined script when hooking up: Men come on to women. Women consent to being kissed. Men get a little more aggressive. Women gently push back. Men pursue further, and so on. Men are the aggressors and women are the gatekeepers. The bottom line is that Traditional flirts not only believe in this script, they practice what they preach. They strictly follow this series of gender-prescribed actions because they strongly believe that this is how it is supposed to happen.

RESEARCH SAYS

Many men think that women who initiate a conversation are seductive and open to having sex.

Role Reversal

As you might imagine, men are much more likely than women to wish that women would make the first move. Many men would be happy to give up their role as aggressor. This means that a truly Traditional flirting style in a man is pretty rare. However, by not being at least somewhat Traditional, men are probably missing out on a lot of potential dates. Without approaching women and being assertive in courtship, a guy is most likely just going to sit in the corner of the bar with only his drink for company. Most women rarely approach men who don't take at least some sort of proactive role. On the other hand, for women, not being at least a little Traditional has real consequences. A woman who is somewhat aggressive can potentially damage her reputation and come off as promiscuous.

COLLECTING THE DATA

The eHarmony Study

Having discovered the five styles, we created a very long survey and sent it to our eHarmony volunteers. We had questions about dating, about long-term relationships, about personality, about flirting success and failures, and about life on the singles scene. Once the survey was created and put online, eHarmony posted a link to the survey in its newsletter in February 2007.

The response was immediate and overwhelming. People couldn't wait to share their experiences with us. Despite its length, 5,020 people completed the entire survey within two weeks! The people who completed the survey were extremely diverse. Although more than two-thirds of eHarmony volunteers were women, this still left us with over 1,500 men. The volunteers ranged in age from 18 to 96 years old and were an average of 40 years old. A little over half were never-married singles, and the rest were divorced, widowed or separated.

The most important goal of this survey was to use all the experiences and attitudes of active eHarmony daters from all walks of life to create a measure of each of the five flirting styles. Using some complicated statistics, we found the best questions to measure each style. This became the original FSI. With some important changes and improvements, these are the same questions that you answered to learn about your own flirting style.

We were very excited about this project. I quickly wrote about the flirting styles in an academic article and the next spring I gave a presentation about the flirting styles to a packed room at the International Communication Association Conference in Montreal, Canada. I then submitted, revised and published the flirting styles in an academic journal called *Communication Quarterly*. But I was only getting started.

The University of Kansas Study

By the time the flirting styles study appeared in print, I was a newly minted assistant professor at the University of Kansas. I thought other people might be interested in knowing more about our flirting styles research. With the help of KU's fantastic Media Relations team, we wrote a press release and created a website where people could take the online FSI and get individualized feedback. I thought this would be a great opportunity to find volunteers to complete a new survey on flirting styles. So, in addition to the FSI website, I created a new survey with all new questions. If people wanted to participate, they could click on a link at the bottom of the page of the online inventory. In the fall of 2010, things got very exciting.

Only two weeks after KU issued the press release in November 2010, 8,500 people had completed the online FSI. By the time

USA TODAY printed a story on flirting styles in December, over 35,000 had discovered their flirting style. After *Time* magazine released a special online Valentine's Day story, over 58,000 people had personalized flirting feedback. There was huge buzz around the flirting styles, and people were very interested in learning more.

At the same time, nearly 4,500 people were volunteering from all over the world to share their dating and flirting experiences on my new survey. Throughout the book, when I refer to the results of this survey, I will call it the FSI Survey. Half of the volunteers were from the United States, and at least three people completed the survey from each of the 50 states and Puerto Rico and Washington, D.C. There were also Canadians, Brits, Australians, New Zealanders and South Africans who participated. The Greeks, Singaporeans, Danes, Mexicans, Croatians, Germans and Chileans also shared their dating and flirting experiences. The FSI was translated into Portuguese for a Brazilian magazine, and I was interviewed on live radio for a program in Bogotá, Colombia. The five flirting styles had gone global!

Looking at who completed the entire FSI Survey, there were several similarities and some differences when compared to the eHarmony study. Like the original survey, about two-thirds were women and single, but the average age was a bit younger, at 32. Because I was no longer using eHarmony volunteers, there were some people who were currently married or in a serious relationship who talked about how their flirting style made a difference in their love life. Thanks to great information provided by the original 5,020 eHarmony users and the 4,500 generous people throughout the world, there is some terrific and one-of-a-kind information that I can pass along to you. In the next chapters, you will learn all about how your flirting style influences every facet of courtship—from where you meet people to how you love once you get into a relationship—all thanks to the shared wisdom of nearly 10,000 daters all over the world.

Finally, as part of the research for this book, I conducted extensive interviews with dozens of active daters who had completed the FSI. From the audio recordings of these interviews, I pulled the best quotes and stories. Throughout the coming chapters, the people I introduce and the quotes that I use are drawn from these interviews. All their identities have been changed, but each came from a real person who completed the Flirting Styles Inventory.

Chapter Two

THE PHYSICAL STYLE

You could say that Aria has game. When she gets ready for a night on the town, Aria is in a zone, blasting music and pumping herself up like an athlete warming up before the big game. She dresses to impress in high heels and a sheer, sexy outfit. On her way out the door, Aria shoots off several texts to her girlfriends, scoping out the best place to start the night out right. When she knows who is going to be there and who is coming with them, she is ready to hit the clubs.

You've probably seen girls like Aria out before. Aria is the girl dancing by the door while the bouncer checks her ID. Before she takes her first step onto the dance floor, she's ready to roll.

Dr. Monica Moore, a pioneering researcher in the science of flirting, went to bars and clubs and recorded the mating signals of women who were open to being approached by men. One of the most common nonverbal signs Dr. Moore found was a woman dancing alone. Maybe you've seen a girl like Aria shake her hips or nod her head while waiting for a drink. Aria's body language says to every guy who looks her way, "You know how to whistle, don't you?"

People think that women rarely approach men and that women simply don't use pickup lines. That is only partly true. According to my FSI Survey, women who are Physical flirts are 31 percent more likely to use a pickup line to start a conversation with a guy than women who are less Physical flirts. Aria knows how to approach cute guys, and she has a plan and even a line ready to go. Normally, a smile or a quick, "Hey, what's up?" will do. If she really wants to get the attention of a particular guy, she might ask if he has a light or what he is drinking. Once she has made contact, she can talk with the best of them. If she sees a guy starting to lose interest or if he keeps to himself too much, she backs out in a hurry. From her perspective, guys who don't show the proper amount of attention are just not worth her time. There are lots of other men who know how to play along.

Aria loves the game of hard to get. She plays it better than most girls. The highlights are:

1. Be interested, even come on strong, if necessary.
2. Back out, be reserved.
3. Make him come and get you.
4. Repeat.

As soon as he looks as if he is about to bail for good, give him one last dose of attention. When someone like Aria plays hard to get, she'll often give a guy a hard time as soon as he is sure she's blowing him off. Aria likes to tease guys about how weak their game is and how they ought to know what girls really want and what girls are really like. She'll laugh as she teaches guys how the game works. Aria loves guys who are down to party and have fun, guys who seem kind of crazy and wild. She likes to go where the action is.

RESEARCH SAYS

In the 1950s, famous social scientist Talcott Parsons identified the "glamour girl" as one who could exert sexual sway over men.

As Seth gets ready for a night out, he spends some time—maybe a little too much time—getting his dark hair arranged just so. (Seth's friends have nicknamed him Vidal because of his obsession with hair products.) After Seth showers and shaves, he spends an hour in front of a mirror admiring and perfecting his look. Maybe he'll do a shot or two and a little manscaping to make sure he is ready for later that night—just in case something good happens. He is always the last one ready to go, but he always looks the freshest out the door.

Seth gives the bar a quick once-over when he arrives, looking for girls who look back. While some men might be embarrassed to be caught checking out an attractive woman, for Seth, if she catches him looking it means she is interested. Better yet, he likes to catch her looking. Eye contact is key for Seth. It is like the blast of a whistle to get the race started. Girls won't walk up to a guy very often (very Physical flirts like Aria are exceptions), and guys typically won't walk up to a girl if he hasn't made eye contact with her first. Getting the female glance is like a written invitation to approach. And Seth knows it.

Once he settles down into a booth surveying the scene, Seth knows how to draw attention to himself. Seth is the guy at the bar who is super-talkative and laughing loudly with his friends. Seth knows intuitively that when he laughs like this, it shows the ladies that he is fun-loving and well-liked by his friends. Laughter in a bar is like a megaphone at a pep rally. It attracts attention and rises above the humdrum chatter of any social scene. Laughter helps get the party started.

One study found that when there are women present—especially girls that the guys find attractive—men change the way they behave. The things those researchers found are pretty noticeable in Seth's flirting style. Seth is the guy leaning back into a booth as if he owns it, with his arms open, his body taking up more space than any of the other guys. Seth doesn't look at his friends while he talks. Maybe you've seen Seth before and you know what he looks like. He surveys the room, while showing that the booth is his territory. He owns that particular corner and just maybe the whole bar, too. Guys who believe (or at least convincingly pretend) that they own whatever place they are in, that this is their party and all the other people there are just guests—these men are truly Physical flirts. This is Seth to a *T*.

When Seth decides to approach a girl, he is very strategic about it. He knows it is no good to approach a girl when she is with her friends. A table of girls is no-go territory. A guy looks like a tool hanging around the outside of a table, trying to find a seat. A guy must look for a better opening. Seth uses the classic buy-her-a-drink strategy, but does it with a twist. If he has made eye contact a couple of times with a girl, he waits until she gets up to get a drink. By paying attention to her movements, Seth can swoop in at the right moment and buy her a drink. It is better still if he is already running a tab. Then there are no interruptions to pay a bartender. Girls rarely go to bars without their friends, but getting them alone is absolutely necessary.

Once the drinks are served, Seth is the chat-up king. As he is talking to a girl, he knows how to keep the conversation going. He knows that people get nervous talking at bars and he finds it a turn-on when girls are nervous; he takes it as a good sign that she wants to make a good impression. Seth likes it when girls are just a little shy. If he sees that, he ups the ante. He throws her a compliment, he leans into her, he brushes her hair off her shoulder—whatever it takes to make her just a little more uncomfortable. For the Physical flirt, this is how it is done.

Cyber-flirting

Physical flirts' communication of attraction extends to their cell phone: they enjoy sexting.

Aria and Seth are perfect examples of the Physical flirting style. Aria and Seth know what they are doing at bars and clubs. They look the part. They know the game. Below is a rundown of what the Physical flirting style is all about.

WHAT IS THE PHYSICAL FLIRTING STYLE?

The Physical style was created to try to capture the essence of flirting from a physical perspective. Academics, Hollywood and *Cosmo* will all tell you that if you want to know if someone is flirting, you should look at her body language. Classic flirting behaviors include the coy smile and shared and prolonged eye contact. These are all part of Physical flirting. This style captures what a person does physically with her body, face and voice, and whether or not she does it well. The Physical flirt isn't shy about letting someone know how she feels. She uses her physicality, nonverbal behavior and physical attractiveness to her advantage. Singles who are Physical flirts recognize this quality in other people and can use their bodies, faces and voice to convey that same romantic desire in return. When people who score high in the Physical flirting style decide to approach their selected target, they feel successful and confident, and they can quickly intimate the possibility of something more. The bottom line: the Physical flirting style is the direct and confident communication of romantic interest.

WHO IS A PHYSICAL FLIRT?

Mostly Women

No matter what their age, women report a higher Physical flirting style than men. Men take a more dominant role in starting

courtship, especially approaching women, introducing themselves and starting conversation. But women often take a leading
role in attracting men's attention through nonverbal signs. When
I found that women were more Physical flirts both in the eHarmony Survey and the FSI Survey, this confirmed what I already
knew. The Physical style is about physicality and nonverbal communication. It is pretty obvious that women have more options
than men when it comes to body language, and that women are
also more capable of using body language and physical attractiveness to flirt than men are. Compared to women, who have
a whole arsenal of outfits (and the accompanying unmention-
ables), makeup choices, nonverbal behaviors and tactics, men
don't have nearly as much at their disposal to attract women
by dress or body language. As the old joke goes, a woman in
nothing but socks is sexy, but a man in nothing but socks is sad.

In Their 30s

Confidence in the Physical communication of romantic interest
is higher in your 30s than at any other time of your life. Younger
daters, between 18 and 24 years old, reported the lowest scores
on Physical flirting style, and scores on the Physical style gradually increased in the late 20s into the 30s. After that, a Physical
flirting style peaks and levels off until your late 30s. The Physical
style declines as a person ages from that point onward. It makes
sense that people become less confident in their physicality and
expression of sexual interest as they age. It could also be due to
other factors, including not being as interested in hooking up and
being more interested in establishing a meaningful connection.

It may be surprising that the Physical flirting style isn't the most common among teenagers and young adults. Although people might think that beauty is wasted on the young, it doesn't appear that the same is true for flirting capability. Turns out that the Physical style is still undeveloped in the college crowd. You could think of college and young adulthood as hard-core flirting training. Going out to party and hooking up is part of college culture. While there isn't a lot of research on flirting among teenagers, the little that is there suggests that they are rather inept at it. Teenagers are still into roughhousing and other teasing, flirtatious games. You might think of these little games as the raw materials from which flirting is sculpted.

RESEARCH SAYS

Teenage boys reported using mock aggression to show romantic interest and flirt. This includes tickling, arm punching, wrestling and bear hugging, growling and biting.

Complementary Styles

The Physical flirting style is most closely linked to the Playful flirting style (see page 81); these two are a common pairing. In Chapter 4, "The Playful Style," I go into more detail about the differences between the two, but, for now, it is enough to know that Physical flirts might use flirting to get a free drink or a little boost to their self-esteem. Physical flirts are rarely Polite flirts, a style that doesn't mesh with the direct approach of the Physical style. Traditional female flirts aren't often Physical flirts, as Traditional women take a more demure role in courtship (Lady Di, not Lady Gaga). But Traditional male flirts like being the aggressor, the suitor and the white knight, so they are often Physical flirts.

Outgoing and in a Good Mood

Personalitywise, Physical flirts are very outgoing and gregarious. They like to hang out with other people and prefer the company of others to being alone or quiet. They are also less likely to experience negative emotions, like sadness, depression and anger. Physical flirts are friendly, outgoing and in a pretty good mood most of the time.

WHERE THE PHYSICAL FLIRT FINDS LOVE

As I explained, there are three different paths to starting a relationship: the Hookup, the First Date and the Known Quantity. People with different flirting styles tend to follow different pathways to romance and find love successfully in different places. You'll flirt more successfully if you go to a place where your flirting style is welcome and acceptable, rather than off-putting and out of place. The Physical flirt's home territory *is* the bar or the club. This is where he has a home field advantage.

To find out more about how flirting style influences where people go to find a boyfriend or girlfriend, in the FSI Survey I asked volunteers where they met their last romantic partner.

The top three locations were: friends and family (25 percent), school (21 percent) and work (16 percent). By way of comparison, only 8 percent had found their last boyfriend or girlfriend at a bar or a club. And most of these people were Physical flirts. Physical flirts were 26 percent more likely to have met their last partner at a bar or club than less Physical flirts. Physical flirts didn't seek out partners through friends and family, school or work. They went to a bar. According to the FSI Survey, nearly half of the men and two-thirds of the women who had met their last partner in a bar or club scored high on the Physical flirting style.

Not surprisingly, Physical flirts *love* being single. If you asked a Physical flirt where to go to meet people, she'd look at you if you were crazy and say, "A bar, of course." They are the ones dragging their friends out over and over again. Lots of people think that it is frustrating to try to meet new people, but the Physical flirt is nearly never frustrated. Just like Seth, they can't imagine why a guy would go to a bar and not try to chat up the ladies. For the Physical flirt, a bar is a place to have fun, meet new people and possibly find some romantic interest; the Physical flirt is sure to keep things light and fun at a bar, careful to avoid conversation that gets too heavy or personal.

THE PHYSICAL FLIRT IS CONFIDENT

The Physical flirt has confidence in spades. The eHarmony Survey showed that more than any other flirting style, the Physical flirt feels successful when she flirts. She feels good about the interaction while it is happening and then looks back on it optimistically when it is over. When talking to someone, she wants to figure out whether or not there is any romantic potential there and the Physical flirt is adept at steering the conversation in that direction. As one Physical flirt that I interviewed explained: "If the conversation goes on to talk about what you're doing later, that's a sign you are looking for more than friends." In the FSI Survey, I asked daters whether they thought they were better at flirting than their friends. Physical flirts said they were. Physical flirts also said they had friends who were good at flirting, too. Physical flirts believe they are the best of the best.

Unlike those who fall into the other four flirting style categories, Physical flirts believe that when men approach and talk to women at a bar, they are flirting. Period. There is no confusion. There is no uncertainty. People who score high on the other flirting styles may wonder what counts as flirting and feel a bit of reasonable doubt. But Physical flirts believe that flirting is happening the moment a guy opens his mouth to talk with a girl. What comes out of his mouth is another matter, but we'll get to that in a second.

The Physical flirt is also the *only* flirting style who will go to a bar or club alone. I found this to be simply amazing because I doubted that anyone really did this. But in the FSI survey, I asked whether or not people would go to a bar alone to meet people. And the Physical flirts said, "Sure, why not?" No other flirting style had the guts to go it alone. So if you ever meet someone at a bar and he is alone, chances are you have a Physical flirt on your hands.

CYBER-FLIRTING

Physical flirts will send more messages, ask more questions and more quickly answer your messages when chatting online.

PHYSICAL TACTICS

Perhaps you have seen VH1's *The Pickup Artist* or read *The Game* by Neil Strauss. If you have, you don't need me to tell you that there is a society of so-called pickup artists out there (*PUAs* as they like to call themselves). PUAs train other guys in how to pick up women. Collectively, they have written several pretty explicit instruction manuals about the sort of things men should do to get women in bed. Endlessly fascinated with this sort of thing, I decided to learn more about it.

I worked with a graduate student (now a PhD in social psychology) named Melanie Canterberry to study the assertive pickup strategies taught in *The Pickup Artist* and exposed in *The Game*. We found that there were three primary strategies: *compete, isolate* and *tease. Compete* means that men should be assertive, pushy and relentless with a woman, whether she is with her friends or even with a boyfriend. It also means that men should be persistent and direct, not taking "No thanks" for an answer. *Isolate* is a group of tactics used to get a woman alone. Just like Seth, guys who attempt to separate a woman from her friends use the isolate tactic. They believe that getting a woman alone is a great way to start a conversation or chat her up. But isolate also means that a man should try to take a woman home or take it to another level physically. This can mean getting a woman out of the bar to someplace more intimate. Finally, *teasing* is typified by the guy who is insulting, obnoxious or just plain mean to women he is interested in. This is also the guy who says, "I'm just kidding" when he is called out by an offended woman for being a jerk. For Physical flirts, these tactics come naturally. They don't need to learn these strategies from PUAs.

Male Physical flirts use competitive pickup tactics all the time and often try to isolate women at bars and clubs. This is how they deliver the message, "I want you." They don't see these behaviors in a negative light at all. They think it is just how men ought to be, and this is how women like to be approached. In no way does this mean that men are learning all their moves from reality TV programs and tell-all memoirs. These tactics are already out there and a highly Physical guy uses them plenty.

You may be wondering, What kind of women find this sort of thing attractive? Like the men who use them, all three of these tactics are enticing to women who are Physical flirts. Furthermore, the direct approach isn't something that applies only to men. Female Physical flirts like Aria know that there is a risk involved in coming on too strong. She has to remind herself to play hard to get sometimes. As one Physical flirt told me: "I have to learn not to be so available. I think I am just too forward sometimes."

This study that Melanie and I did also matches up well with the eHarmony Survey. There, we found that people who scored high in the Physical style would have personal and private conversations with someone to show interest. During that conversation, they were flirting the whole time. They didn't waste time with polite conversation. The Physical flirt has a whole approach down pat: she goes into a club prepared, she scans the scene for interest, she finds some available people to talk to and, soon enough, she is chatting up a romantic prospect over a drink.

How to Spot a Physical Flirt

1. Soon after meeting you, a Physical flirt will clearly show you if he is attracted to you.
2. If you meet online, Physical flirts feel comfortable disclosing personal details, and will want to meet you face-to-face as soon as possible.
3. Physical flirts will (mis)interpret your friendliness as flirtatiousness.
4. Whether a man or a woman, a Physical flirt will be more aggressive, assertive, competitive and dominant, compared to any other flirting style.
5. A Physical woman will use a pickup line at a bar or lay on the flattery on a date.
6. Physical flirts are incredibly confident that other people want them and find them attractive. They are the only style that feels so self-assured.
7. A Physical flirt will go alone to a bar to pick up attractive strangers.
8. A Physical flirt will talk about his workout habits or athletic accomplishments when first meeting someone.

9. A Physical flirt might be juggling multiple dating partners at the same time.
10. A Physical flirt will fall in love fast!

THE PHYSICAL STYLE AND SEX

Sex on the Brain

A person's flirting style says a lot about the way she sees and understands sex and how quickly she (hopes to) end up in bed. In the eHarmony Survey, we were able to determine a couple of key features of the Physical style's love life.

Physical flirts move fast. This is partly because Physical flirts know how to pick up the opposite sex and they spend quite a bit of time in the bar scene, which isn't exactly a hot spot for developing long-term relationships. But the Physical flirt also feels more attracted more quickly. Physical flirts say that they experience romantic attraction immediately after meeting someone. This was simply not the case for any other flirting style. This means that, on a fundamental level, the Physical flirting style is related to feeling sexually attracted to other people often and intensely.

QUOTABLE

"I think I'm being friendly with someone and I'll sit in their lap. They think I'm flirting with them."

—Singer Kylie Minogue

Some time ago, Dr. Linda Koeppel and her colleagues found that some people think that flirting is basically a reflection of uncontrollable, underlying sexual urges, that seductiveness and promiscuousness come part and parcel with flirting. People who see flirting this way believe that people's true sexual desires "leak out" of their bodies unawares. Each flirtatious body movement and smile is merely the body's way of saying, "I'm sexually attracted to you." According to Dr. Koeppel, for those who think this way, flirting always has sexual meanings. For example, when they watch two strangers interacting, they "read" much more sexual attraction and desire into the interaction than is really there—they believe the strangers really want each other sexually. To me, this research sounds exactly like the Physical style of flirting, and the eHarmony Survey accords with this perspective.

We found that the Physical flirt sees flirting between two people everywhere, just like those in Dr. Koeppel's study. In fact, they think people are flirting with *them* wherever they go. Oddly enough, they are undeterred by being wrong. More than any other flirting style, Physical flirts have the following experience: at first they think someone is flirting with them, but then afterward find out they were totally wrong. But, interestingly, they don't care. Even more, they rarely have the opposite problem—that they try to be forward and people don't get the hint. This means Physical flirts have no trouble conveying their romantic interest. Just like Aria and Seth, they are obvious and direct. Although they might sometimes seem a little pushy or aggressive, it is just the way they are on a fundamental level.

> ### CYBER-FLIRTING
> When chatting online, Physical flirts think the conversation is going so well that they overestimate how much their partner is flirting with them—just as they do in real life.

CASUAL SEX AND PHYSICALITY

Let's take a trip back to the heady days of the famous and pioneering sex researcher Alfred Kinsey. Over 60 years ago, Kinsey introduced the world to a concept he called sociosexuality. This was the idea that people are either open to casual sex or would prefer sex within the comfort of a romantic relationship. On one side of the continuum, people are promiscuous and on the other side, they want a relationship first, then sex. Some recent research by a pair of German researchers linked flirting with an interest in no-strings-attached sex. What they found is that how you flirt has a lot to do with whether you'd prefer a one-night stand or sex after some get-to-know-you time. People who were open to one-night stands laughed and smiled more when talking with an attractive stranger. Their eyes told a similar story. Flirtatious men who were also open to short-term sex tended to stare at an attractive female directly and intensely. Flirtatious women who were open to short-term sex tended to lean forward and flash a coy glance. How you flirt has a lot to do with your sexual history as well.

Now what does this have to do with the Physical style? According to the FSI Survey, those who have a Physical style of flirting have had *a lot* of sexual experiences. They have had more partners in general and more one-night stands specifically. Interestingly, women with a more Physical flirting style have more sexual desire, too. This means that for women who are very Physical flirts, their flirting style *is* indeed an indication of their underlying sexual urges. This matches up very nicely with the eHarmony Survey, which found that Physical flirts experience more sexual chemistry than other flirting styles. They might even use sex to try to hook a boyfriend or girlfriend. According to the FSI Survey, Physical flirts were 25 percent more likely to use sex to try to start a long-term relationship. Sex may simply come first for the Physical flirt. They feel it, show it and might use it to jump-start a relationship.

RESEARCH SAYS

The most common reason for engaging in casual sex is for its own sake: sexual pleasure, pure and simple.

Physical flirts have more sex, feel sexual attraction faster, experience heightened sexual chemistry and think that people are flirting with them everywhere they go. No wonder they have no trouble getting their message across!

THE PHYSICAL FLIRT AND CHEATING

Volunteers in the FSI Survey were asked whether or not they flirt with other people while they are in a committed relationship and whether they date multiple people at once. Physical flirts were 33 percent more likely to admit to flirting with other potential partners while in a long-term relationship, and Physical flirts were 36 percent more likely to date several people at the same time. Since they see flirting as something that happens everywhere, they read sexuality and physical attraction into everyday situations. For Physical flirts, it is hard to just turn off their flirting switch once they get a boyfriend or girlfriend. It is hard for them to give up on what they see is a good thing—constant sexual interest communicated to and from the opposite sex.

Highly Physical flirts probably cheat more, too. Physical flirts are more likely to have had a lot of past sexual experiences. As I like to say, the best predictor of future behavior is past behavior. There is good reason to believe that this abundant sexual desire will translate into cheating on their romantic partner. As one researcher put it, desirable people who are open to romance are often approached by strangers for no-strings-attached sex. More opportunities for sex mean more opportunities to cheat.

RESEARCH SAYS

Don't try to convert a guy into being interested in a long-term relationship by sleeping with him—it doesn't tend to work.

RELATIONSHIPS AND LOVE

Let's look at how Physical flirts experience love. The Love Attitudes scale was created to figure out what people think about love and how they experience love in their relationships. These researchers identified six different love attitudes, and they pinned down the experiences unique to each one. In the FSI Survey, I looked at how the flirting styles matched up with the love attitudes. Physical flirts have two competing views of love.

On one hand, they are very committed to *eros*. This version of love says love is a deep well of physical chemistry and attraction. For erotic lovers, true love is found in the love of two people who are meant to be together. On the other hand, Physical flirts also tend to imitate the love of the wolf—*ludic* love. This version of love sees love as a game played between two people (and maybe a third party, to spark some jealousy and excitement). We know that people with a *ludic* attitude about love enjoy hooking up on a regular basis. They are out on the town looking for a relationship, but they are also out on the town after they get into a relationship. Having a relationship isn't going to tie them down. For the Physical flirt, an intense romantic relationship is filled with passion and drama. Sadly, it might be drama that they created.

Physical flirts rate their last major relationship as being very important and meaningful. They describe that last relationship as one in which they established a strong emotional connection. This means they have good reason to try to make their relationships work—they have strong and meaningful ones. The tricky part for Physical flirts is that they are pulled in opposing directions. Their love for their partner is driven by passion and chemistry, which is very satisfying and helps to forge a tighter bond. But it is also driven by game playing, which can destabilize and frustrate a relationship. Physical flirts can feel close to someone nearly immediately, but they also start a fight at the first sign that a partner is losing interest. See how their way of having a committed romantic relationship closely matches Aria's suggestions about how to keep a guy interested? Attract, pull away, attract, pull away and repeat. Without a doubt, how you flirt tells a lot about how you love someone, too.

PHYSICAL FLIRTS IN LOVE

For Hannah and Tim it all started at a New Year's Eve party. Our two lovers had never met before that night. Fortunately, this party offered our two Physical flirts a golden opportunity to strut their stuff. As fate would have it, one of their friends at the party had received as a Christmas gift a board game in which players had to answer questions about their sex life and sexual fantasies. The night was young, and the group of friends thought it might be a fun way to pass the time before they hit the clubs. Before I tell you how the game turned out, I want to tell you a bit more about our star-crossed lovers.

Hannah hadn't had many serious relationships. She had been a single girl long enough to know what to do if a guy seemed interested. If he came on strong, she would brush him off. Tim was different. He was comfortable in his own skin. Even though he had to respond to some pretty racy questions, he never seemed embarrassed by his own sexual desires or experiences. As the night went on and the game got a little out of hand, Tim turned the game into an opportunity to show Hannah that he was interested in *her*.

For Tim, Hannah was special because she was fun, easy to be around and, above all, comfortable with herself, no matter how crazy things got. Tim thought she was extremely hot because she didn't just play the game, she took the time to develop each answer into a great story of her exploits. Even when playing a board game with relative strangers, she was unafraid. She was sarcastic and clever—you could never tell if the story was actually true. Even though some guys would find Hannah's sense of humor a tad too sarcastic or too dirty, Tim loved it. She could make and take a joke better than any woman he had ever met.

The game had gotten stale and the friends got ready to take off to the club to ring in the New Year. Hannah and Tim now had a ton of ammunition. At the bar, Tim started off as he often did with women; he tried to make a few jokes at Hannah's expense. But Hannah wasn't having it. She threw each comment right back at him. So Tim tried again, turning up the charm. He bought Hannah his favorite shot for girls, a slippery nipple. It usually made them a little uncomfortable and could start a conversation. Hannah called him on it, saying, "Pretty predictable, don't you think?" She said all of it with a smile to let him know he shouldn't stop trying. Before long, the two of them were in a zone. No one else was there that night. Hannah had no problem letting him know how she felt. Within 30 minutes of getting to know her at the bar, Tim knew what kind of woman Hannah was and he loved it.

Tired of talking, the two spent the evening on the dance floor, barely talking to their friends. They were always up for the next great song, no matter how tired everyone else got. New Year's passed and the night wore down. In the wee small hours of the morning, they went for food with their friends. Tim played it cool, but before he had a chance to do the same, Hannah asked for his number, teasing him about how long it took for him to get around to it.

Tim and Hannah talked and texted for a week or two before they hung out again. Their attraction to one another—felt so keenly that first night—grew into something more serious. They were physically compatible but also had compatible personalities. And they had fun together. For Hannah and Tim, their Physical flirting style translated into an ability to show their love and passion clearly and directly in their relationship. You could say they spoke the same love language.

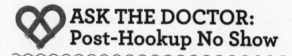 ## ASK THE DOCTOR: Post-Hookup No Show

Dear Dr. Hall,

I've been hanging out with this guy in my group of friends for a while, and I have a crush on him. Last weekend, I hooked up with him at a drunken party. I thought that he was into me, but now I feel like he's been blowing me off ever since we hooked up. What's his flirting style?

—Jess (High on Sincere and Physical Style, Low on Traditional)

That's a tough question, but I think what you are really asking me is, What's his deal? How should I read him? One thing that I can tell you is that women are much more likely than men to think that hooking up is a pathway toward a long-term relationship. This is a tough situation in your case, particularly because you wanted this to turn out a certain way. You hooked up with him knowing you were attracted to him, and hoping it would turn out well. From your flirting style, I can tell that you probably had no trouble getting him interested in you. You easily communicate sexual attraction, you know how to seek an emotional connection and you have no problem approaching guys. I'd bet you pushed the fast-forward button on courtship. It isn't that a long-term relationship can't get started now; it's just that in your mind you have already stepped on the gas pedal.

What about him? Well, you haven't given me much to go on to try to guess his flirting style, but we know three things: you hooked up (drunkenly), you knew him beforehand and he isn't acting fast. I'll give you two reads on this, and you can choose which is a better fit. The first possibility is that he is a Traditional flirt. The fact that he knew you well before hooking up and he isn't following through particularly quickly is very Traditional. The trouble with this is that Traditional men find Traditional women to be most attractive, but you are clearly not Traditional. This may have been a turnoff for him. My other read on this situation is that he is a Playful flirt. You said it seemed as if he was into you, too. It's possible that he used his charms to get you to like him, but he was never really interested in anything more than a hookup.

Truth is, these early stages of relationships are tough for a lot of people. Nearly all of us have been in a situation where our own romantic interests didn't match our crush's level of interest. The upshot for you is that you've got a great set of skills based on your flirting style that will help you move on if this guy isn't the one. And, if anything, you can learn something from this situation. Not everyone is going to move as fast, feel as close and enjoy that chemistry as quickly as you are. Just because guys aren't as quick to show their affection doesn't mean they don't feel that way, too.

Chapter Three

THE POLITE STYLE

Noah is a charming, intelligent and an exceedingly pleasant guy. He is relaxed and casual when he talks to people; he is a great conversationalist. But Noah is not so good at having one-on-one conversations with people he has just met, especially girls, and *especially* at bars.

Noah is a fish out of water at clubs and bars. If he is just going out with his friends, it is a different matter. He loves hanging out with friends to catch up. And Noah *has* met people at bars—lots of people, in fact. He is that guy who makes sure that the friends of friends are included in the conversation. He wants to make sure nobody is left out. Because he typically hangs with the guys, he is more likely to include a friend's girlfriend in the conversation than to pick up on a girl who is actually available.

Part of Noah's problem is that he just doesn't get how guys do it. How do they approach women at bars, especially attractive girls? Like an audience member at a play, Noah watches men approach women, drink and talk, dance seductively and sometimes go home together. To him, the way guys and girls meet up at bars might as well be a foreign mating ritual.

For Noah, even good opportunities go to waste. One time he was out with his friends, celebrating his birthday. Noah was in rare form—talkative, boisterous and enjoying the lack of inhibitions caused by one too many drinks. A cute girl offered to buy a drink for him when she learned it was his birthday—and Noah turned her down! He said, "Thank you very much, but I already have a drink." The funny thing is he didn't mean to blow her off. From his point of view, he was just being polite. He knew his limit, and he didn't want her to waste her money. It never occurred to him that she might have been flirting with him. In fact, if his friends hadn't mercilessly teased him for weeks upon weeks about this, he wouldn't have thought he had done anything wrong. He was being quite gentlemanly, in fact.

The one time Noah decided to play the game and try flirting in a bar, it was a disaster. He finally worked up the courage to talk to an attractive woman, sipping a drink by herself. He introduced himself, but he hadn't really planned his next move after hello, so there was a long, painful, awkward silence, until she said, "I gotta go. My friend is here. It was nice meeting you." And that was it. Maybe she really did have to go. Or maybe she felt the silence as keenly as he did.

Noah's other problem is that he has a strong dislike—you could even say a hatred—of overtly sexual comments or aggressive come-ons. In his mind, girls mean it when they say that they don't like it when skeezy men come on strong or get too aggressive. In his mind, girls do not want to be touched at all (yes, girls, believe it or not, these guys do exist!). Noah believes that a guy has to respect a girl's personal space, especially when she doesn't know him. Out of respect, Noah keeps his distance when he talks with girls, especially girls he really likes. He consciously maintains good eye contact and listens carefully to what she has to say, but he keeps a comfortable distance from her. From Noah's perspective, even a compliment might be a little too much. Everyone hates cheesy pickup lines, right? Be respectful, be sweet and be charming. To Noah, anything more than that is suspect, in bad taste or just plain rude.

Noah is a good-looking, high-quality guy. Noah's friends think he is a good catch. Now, if he could only manage to get himself caught. It isn't that Noah isn't interested in sex, either. He puts girls on a pedestal. He actually thinks to himself, *This is somebody's daughter. I should treat her well.* As a consequence, he has never taken a girl home the first night he met her or even intended to do so. What he really wants is a good conversation. Through that conversation, Noah is showing he cares about her and wants to know more about who she is and what matters to her. He wants her to see him that way, too. For Noah, that is how flirting is done right. It has always been this way for him and, in his mind, it is how it ought to be for everyone.

How to Spot a Polite Flirt

1. If you are friends with someone for a while and he starts flirting with you out of the blue, then he is probably a Polite flirt.
2. You'll find Polite flirts hiding out, talking to their friends at a bar, seemingly uninterested in meeting new people.
3. A Polite flirt will pay really close attention to what you have to say while getting to know you—well before going on a date.
4. A Polite woman works hard to protect her reputation.
5. A Polite guy is less aggressive, assertive and dominant than other men might be, but that doesn't mean he isn't interested. It is his way of showing respect.
6. A man with a Polite flirting style will not directly compliment or comment about a woman's appearance.
7. Polite flirts find obvious and direct flirting annoying—especially pickup lines.
8. A Polite guy will talk about his long-term relationship goals on a first date.
9. Polite flirts are honest, both in general and about their relationship history, because they probably have nothing to hide.
10. A Polite flirt might call to make sure you got home safely or send you a thank-you text the day after a date.

Long ago, Erin figured out that the bar and club scene just wasn't for her. She had always been a bit shy, preferring the company of friends in more intimate settings. Her friends and family, strangers even, tell her that she is one of the nicest people that they know. But going to bars just never worked for Erin. Wisely, she stopped trying to make her flirting style work in such an uncomfortable place. Instead, she tried to get to know potential boyfriends in the most comfortable place she knew—her church groups.

But Erin has since learned the drawbacks of this approach. She knows everyone at church functions. True to character, she is incredibly nice to the people there. Erin sees the best in people and tries to treat everyone with respect and kindness. She always has a big smile on her face and is good-natured and forgiving toward everyone. There is no question that this helps her make friends and keep them. But this isn't a good way to communicate romantic interest. Even the guys she is interested in can't tell that she likes them any more than as a friend. No one knows that she cares about any single person more than anyone else. When everyone feels special, no one is especially special.

Sometimes Erin tries to be a little more assertive than usual. Last spring, she was part of an organizing committee for an Earth Day event. She was coordinating the efforts of several churches and lots of volunteers, but one particular guy caught her attention. Matt was a local youth minister. He was incredibly patient and seemed sincerely interested in what people had to say. Erin made sure she took the time to talk with Matt whenever he was around. She wanted to make sure he saw that she liked being around him and was having fun working with him. Unfortunately, that wasn't quite enough to get the message across. Earth Day came and went, lots of trash got recycled and saplings were planted in droves, but nothing romantic came of it. They'd still see each other around afterward, and the pair always stopped to chat. But neither made any move to show interest beyond that respectful formality.

It went along this way until one of Erin's friends stepped in. Apparently, Matt was interested in Erin, too. He had liked her for a long time, but he didn't tell anyone, much less Erin. Luckily for Erin, Matt kept asking about her, "How is Erin? What is she up to these days?" Erin's friend got the picture and tipped Erin off. Even after that, Erin and Matt were far from getting their relationship off the ground.

It would be another year before the two of them actually went out for something resembling a date. And they both took time to follow up. Erin didn't think it was appropriate to put herself out there sexually. For her, that included asking Matt out, calling him too frequently or trying to dress suggestively in the least. Erin made an effort to look nice whenever they spent time together, but never wore anything she wouldn't wear to church. She felt that if Matt didn't appreciate the person she was and what she usually wore, they probably wouldn't be a good fit anyway.

As Noah's and Erin's stories illustrate, the Polite flirt is somewhere between utterly baffled and strongly annoyed by the world of flirting. Despite this unwillingness to actively pursue romance, fundamentally, the Polite style is still a style of flirting. The Polite flirt still wants to find love and be with someone special. Although it takes some time, Polite flirts are good at being in love once they get there.

WHAT IS THE POLITE FLIRTING STYLE?

The Polite style embraces politeness, refuses to engage in inappropriate or obviously sexual behavior, diligently follows courtship rules and adopts a cautious approach to relationship initiation. Polite flirts find all the unintended consequences of flirting—looking needy, trying too hard, embarrassing oneself, losing control or appearing too promiscuous—simply not worth it. From their perspective, the whole thing is even a little offensive. They don't like it when someone else aggressively flirts with them, either. The Polite flirt feels that people who act that forward are being rude or are just interested in sex. A Polite woman might say, "A man is only interested in one thing," when she explains why she turned down a stranger who offered to buy her a drink. Even when someone special catches the Polite flirt's eye, his first impulse is to be careful, kind and cautious.

The important part about all this is that it doesn't mean that they don't want to develop physical chemistry or end up in a sexual relationship eventually. In fact, they badly want to be in love and in a committed relationship so they can enjoy sexual intimacy. They want to be in love, and respect relationships so much that they don't want their ideals polluted by the ugly, aggressive or unpleasant aspects of flirting. As a consequence, a nonsexual approach is preferred and forward or direct actions are unwelcome.

WHO IS A POLITE FLIRT?

Women

The fairer sex tends to favor the Polite style much more than men do. Undoubtedly, it is to women's advantage to develop a more Polite style. Men are more likely than women to misinterpret signs of sexual interest as being seductive, rather than friendly. Women are much more likely to be sexually harassed and sexually coerced by men. These things may inspire women to develop a keen distaste for overly aggressive men and to favor a more cautious approach to courtship. In addition, if women are too aggressive, people might think they are promiscuous or morally corrupt. As a consequence, there are more female Polite flirts than there are males of this type.

On the other hand, let's not overstate the difference between men and women. There are lots of men who are very Polite flirts. In fact, both the eHarmony and the FSI Survey showed that the Polite style is the second most common style of all (after Sincere). This second-place finish was true for both men and women equally. Like Noah, men know that women might find it off-putting and irritating to be picked up aggressively. Men are aware that many women don't like it when men are too physically forward. Men who pay attention to the plight of their female friends want to be part of the solution not part of the problem.

The Over-40 Crowd

The fact that this style is more common among both men and women over 40 years old is probably a generational thing as well as a consequence of developing a more mature approach to dating. Individuals aged 40 and over have much more formal rules about social grace—courtship and flirting included. And many Polite flirts developed their flirting style when they first started dating or first took a beau to a drive-in movie. There is also the issue of just growing up—the Polite flirting style is a more mature way to flirt than the way teenagers do with their wrestling, pinching and punching mode of flirting.

Complementary Styles

If you are a Polite flirt, you are probably also a Traditional flirt (see page 133) and a Sincere flirt (see page 105). People who are slow-paced and cautious in romance seek an emotional and sincere connection with others, and feel that men and women ought to be gentlemanly and ladylike during courtship. In particular, Polite women are more often Traditional flirts. If you are a man with a Polite style, you are even a more Sincere flirt. What unites these three styles is a concern for avoiding the more sexual and carefree aspects of dating. The Polite flirt seeks a connection through polite and proper interaction, not through pickup lines at a "meat market." Both men and women who score high in the Polite style tend to score low on the Physical style. Erin and Noah, who are both cautious, rule-governed and indirect, don't communicate their romantic desire with the same game playing and seductiveness as Aria and Seth, from Chapter 2, "The Physical Style."

> ### CYBER-FLIRTING
>
> Polite flirts will be really up front about their past relationships in their online profile, in part because they are honest by disposition and in part because they have nothing to hide.

Decorous, Nice and a Little Shy

People who score high on the Polite style are concerned about decorum and have a generally pleasant and agreeable disposition toward others. They like to have everything happen at the right time and in the right place. They know to follow up each important interaction or event with a thank-you note or a phone call. They are concerned about their friends and make sure that they are there in their time of need. They are also a bit introverted. Polite flirts don't need to be the center of attention. In social interactions, they would prefer things to be a bit more controlled and formal. Polite flirts possess an honorable disposition. They are true to who and what they are, no matter what the circumstances. They strictly adhere to their values, and they won't change their mind from place to place or person to person. This means they can sometimes come off as rather rigid and somewhat inflexible to others, but from their point of view this is true and right. It is honest, and honesty is always the best policy.

> ### THE SURVEY SAYS
>
> Although there are many things they won't do for love, Polite flirts can be real charmers when they are into someone.

WHERE THE POLITE FLIRT FINDS LOVE

When I wrote about home turf in Chapter 1, "The Five Flirting Styles," I told you that there were three main pathways to romance: the Hookup, the Known Quantity and the First Date. Without a doubt, Polite flirts do not wish to take the hookup route! Like Noah, they border on *hating* it. As you may have guessed, the Polite style is best suited to traveling the Known Quantity route and, to a lesser extent, the First Date path.

Dreading the Club

The Polite style treats the club scene and the hookup culture that it breeds like a bad part of town. They will drive out of the way to avoid it. To them, the singles scene is just no fun. They believe that no one finds true love at a club. They are even suspicious of couples who met there to begin with. Secretly, they are certain that a relationship started at a club is doomed. If they do end up at a bar, it is only because a friend dragged them there.

Once they are at a bar, Polite flirts like to hide out in the corner. If you have ever complained about how loud music makes it impossible to talk to someone at clubs, then you are probably a Polite flirt. Even if they see an attractive stranger, Polite flirts won't approach. Like Noah, even when they are really interested in someone, they have to psych themselves up to make the first move. It isn't just because they are introverted and don't like being around other people. They are basically offended by flirting at bars in general. Of all the flirting styles, the Polite flirt is most likely to agree with this statement: No one can make a sincere connection when others are on the prowl. To Polite flirts, the bar and club scene is all about trolling for sexual conquests.

And, my goodness, do they hate overly assertive people! As much as the Playful flirt thinks that being competitive or trying to get someone alone is a *good* idea, the Polite flirt thinks it is a *bad* idea. For these types of flirting tactics, the Playful and Polite styles are complete opposites. Most of all, they hate the teasing and being teased tactic. Far and away, this is the flirting style that recoils at the mere sight of someone being picked on or playfully joked with as a form of flirting. Polite female flirts hate it when guys do it, and Polite male flirts would never do it to a woman, especially one they are interested in. If you have ever been irritated by a guy who thinks it is a good idea to tease a woman to show his interest, you are probably a Polite flirt. But the true test is this: if you have ever said, "I just don't understand why any woman would like that," then you are definitely a Polite flirt. Polite flirts are so suspicious of disingenuous and manipulative tactics that they even hate cheesy but harmless pickup lines. For the Polite flirt, "Heaven must be missing an angel" is as offensive as "What are the chances of you and me making out tonight?" To them, all of it is just garbage.

THE SURVEY SAYS

Hitting on someone does not make Polite flirts feel attractive. They don't feel sexier doing it, and they don't feel sexier when other people do it to them.

Church has a singles scene?

It is not just Erin who thinks that church is a good place to meet people. Because they were once the focus of social and community life, houses of worship used to play a much stronger role in courtship in America than they do now. Houses of worship used to be the place where people came together, where families mingled, and where young people met each other under the watchful and protective gaze of their parents and God. These days, religious establishments are still important in bringing people together and finding a potential husband or wife, but not nearly as much as they used to be. According to the FSI Survey, only 2.4 percent had met their most recent romantic partner at a church, a synagogue or some other religious establishment. What was really amazing was that Polite flirts were 35 percent more likely to find someone at church! The Polite style was the only flirting style that looked for love in church.

CYBER-FLIRTING

When chatting online, Polite women are good at making their partners like them.

Online

A small number of Polite flirts also use the internet to meet someone. Polite flirts (compared to less Polite flirts) are about 10 percent more likely to have used the internet to find their last boyfriend or girlfriend. This makes sense, given the fact that more introverted people find the internet to be a welcome place to chat with strangers. Chat rooms, instant messaging and email give introverted people time to formulate carefully constructed and meaningful messages. These online tools give Polite flirts a chance to be polite and charming, and by meeting online they circumvent the potential stress of face-to-face interaction.

School

To a much lesser degree, the Polite flirt seeks romance at school, including college. Although school is a very common place to meet future husbands and wives, the Polite flirt is 10 percent more likely to have met someone in school.

CYBER-FLIRTING

Polite men will err on the side of appropriate and innocuous when chatting on IM—no racy stuff for them.

Known Quantity

What ties these places together? They are all places that give you a chance to slowly and carefully develop a romantic relationship. They are places where romance develops along the path of the Known Quantity. Like some Ang Lee film about long-pining lovers waiting for the perfect time to finally be united, Polite flirts attend church and classes at school with the same patient regard they have for love.

How do I know that Polite flirts are so patient? Well, there are some pretty clear signs. First, they typically know someone for a long time before they develop a relationship with that person. They are more likely to flirt with someone *after* they consider that person a friend. For the Polite flirt, friendship is a good pathway to romance. Take Erin, for example. It was only after forging a strong connection with Matt that she acted on her desire, and even then she was careful. Polite flirts are patient because they typically don't meet a lot of possible candidates. Compared with other flirting styles, Polite flirts were romantically interested in fewer people in the past year. Even if they meet someone with relationship potential, they are less likely to flirt with that person than is someone with any other flirting style! This means that even though they meet very few potential boyfriends or girlfriends, they don't do anything about it—at least not at any speed. Instead, they wait to express their love until the relationship is fully developed. They don't want to act unless they are sure.

THE SURVEY SAYS

Polite flirts will not flirt when they are in a relationship, if there isn't relationship potential or if they don't feel attraction. If they are flirting with you, you must really be something special.

SEX AND LOVE

When people flirt, they are at the very first stages of falling in love. Any journey, no matter how long, begins with a single step. How you flirt influences how fast or slow you take those first steps. Polite flirts take little baby steps, and even those steps are taken slowly and cautiously. People with different flirting styles differ in the way they want to be loved and in the way they show love once they're in a relationship. Polite flirts treasure love and believe so strongly in it that they don't want to be casual about it.

RESEARCH SAYS

Because of the way they fall in love, Polite flirts are very unlikely to hook up with a stranger.

Relationship First, Then Sex

The Polite flirt is the strictest adherent to the rule that sex should occur *only* in the context of a relationship. In fact, Polite flirts are the only flirting style who would never use sex as a possible way into a committed relationship. In fact, those who are high on the Polite flirting style are 26 percent less likely to try a sex-first strategy of starting a relationship.

As you might imagine, Polite flirts have very strict rules about sex. Compared to the other flirting styles, they have fewer past sexual partners. When very Polite flirts are asked how many one-night stands they have had, they nearly always answer "none" (or maybe just one). They don't tend to fantasize about having new sexual partners or relationships. For the Polite flirt, sex isn't on the brain.

However, it is important to keep in mind that it isn't that they don't want sex *at all*. It is just that they believe that sex can only be truly appreciated in the context of a committed relationship. And they are not alone in thinking this way. They desperately want to be in love and are extremely committed to having a real, meaningful relationship. That is their MO. So they take their time to discover and cultivate romantic attraction and love. They may know someone for months or years before they start a relationship with that person.

Research Says

Although people think that there is a huge decline in romantic relationships for the young, and that young people are more likely to engage in casual sex, 81 percent of young people have sex in the context of a committed relationship.

Love Me Do

Once they are finally in a relationship, they are seriously, seriously committed to love. When the FSI Survey asked volunteers to describe their attitudes about love, the results showed that Polite flirts take all that bottled-up flirting energy and put it into becoming an ideal lover. Polite flirts believe that all things can be borne for love. They believe that two lovers endure hardships for each other and make many sacrifices to keep love strong.

Polite flirts are pragmatic about love because they are in it for the long haul. The Polite flirt believes that love is best illustrated by a couple who stays married for 50 years. Love is exemplified by two people who can raise children together, who become intertwined in a family and who successfully navigate the troubled waters of life, family and work. Importantly, the Polite flirt believes that love is about forming a partnership between friends. Polite is the only flirting style associated with the belief that love is—above all things—a gradually growing and developing friendship. The Polite flirt is a very serious and committed lover.

Because You Know I Love You

Not surprisingly, these feelings about love were also reflected in the eHarmony Survey. In that study, Polite flirts described their last romantic relationship as very important and meaningful. In that relationship, both partners felt strongly committed to each other. It wasn't through sexual chemistry, physical attraction or deep emotional connection that this relationship grew. It was from an intense and strong sense of loyalty, commitment and love. Love born in friendship, commitment and self-sacrifice produces an intense feeling of intimacy and companionship.

QUOTABLE

"Whoever loves above all the approach of love will never know the joy of attaining it."

—Antoine de Saint-Exupéry, French author and poet

POLITE FLIRTS IN LOVE

In the days before Facebook, instant messaging and email, people wrote things to each other on pieces of paper, put them in envelopes, bought stamps and trusted a postal carrier to deliver the message. Shocking, isn't it? It was much slower, but there was something very personal about it. Without a doubt, it took *a lot* more work than electronic correspondence. You could see the errors and effort put into hand-writing that letter. You could see the person's penmanship, spelling and storytelling—warts and all. A letter was tangible and real.

I would like to share a story of two Polite flirts who found each other through the exchange of letters. Madeline was home from college for the summer and her mother wanted her to meet a new doctor at the hospital where her mother worked. The doctor, Richard, was eight years older than Madeline and he had been single for a long time as he labored through medical school and residency. Madeline's mother was a bit of a busybody at the hospital, and she was absolutely *charmed* by Richard. He was sweet and sincere. Kind and confident. And did she mention to Madeline that he was single?

Madeline reluctantly agreed to her mother's plan to meet for lunch at the hospital, and then to casually wander by Richard's office to say hello. Madeline was absolutely sure this was *not* going to work. Her mother was a notorious matchmaker with limited success to show for it. The last thing this college girl wanted was to be set up with some older guy, even if he was a young doctor. She was sure he was going to be as stuffy and boring as he was educated.

When Madeline and her mother stopped by his office, Richard was very welcoming. He asked all the right questions. He was kind and very polite. But he was also a bit distracted and seemed to be in a hurry. Nonetheless, he invited Madeline to come back and visit if she came again to see her mother at work. Madeline was quite cool toward Richard. It wasn't that she didn't think that Richard was handsome; she thought he had a classic tall, dark and handsome look about him. She enjoyed the fact that he was so kind and respectful. It was just that she didn't trust her mother's taste in men. It wasn't love at first sight, but it was a start.

When Madeline got back to school, she was surprised to find a letter from Richard waiting for her. In it, he apologized for his rudeness and rush. He asked Madeline about herself, about college and about her family. He spoke of his own time in school and at his new job, and wondered whether and when she might be in town again. Madeline didn't write back. That is, until her mother called and asked why she hadn't. Apparently, Madeline's mother had given Richard her address, and was dying to know whether he had written (and what he wrote—if Madeline would *please* share some details). Her mother was simply appalled that Madeline hadn't written back. "I thought I taught you better than that," she scolded.

Eventually, Madeline wrote back. And Richard did, too. Throughout the year, they wrote back and forth. They missed each other over Christmas because Richard was tied up with other obligations. Although they didn't write frequently, they kept in touch purposefully. Madeline thought that they had become pen pals, friends even, but certainly nothing more.

Despite her own growing affection for and interest in Richard, she kept it to herself. She certainly kept it well concealed from her mother's prying.

By the time she came home for the summer, she was very excited to see Richard—even a little nervous and anxious. They met again in his office under the pretext of Madeline visiting her mother. Richard, again in a hurry, was startled to see her there. He seemed excited, but when he extended his hand to greet her formally, Madeline was a little disappointed. She thought, *I guess he was only a pen pal after all*. Then, on her way out the door, he asked if she might like to have dinner with him sometime. "Very soon, I hope," he added. Somewhat startled, she steadied herself and said, "Yes."

At dinner, Madeline dressed conservatively, of course. She was careful not to be too assertive, and she minded her manners. Richard was charming and completely pleasant. But he never let on during dinner that he was interested in much more than friendship. Madeline struggled to understand what they were doing out together that night, but she was unwilling to press the issue. At the end of the evening and at long last, Richard asked if she might like to go out again. Madeline blushed, and said, "I was starting to think you weren't interested." Richard replied with a smile, "What do you think I was doing with all those letters?"

When Polite flirts find love, it may take a long time to get started, but it tends to be long-lasting.

ASK THE DOCTOR: A Philanthropist Looking for Love

Dear Dr. Hall,

I've been volunteering for a soup kitchen for about two years now. Some of the volunteers are regulars who have become good friends, but every once in a while someone new shows up. A few weeks ago, someone very special came. Mary is awesome—friendly, sweet, outgoing and really funny. She is also super-physical. She gives hugs to everyone and she even pulled the keys out of my pants pocket so she could open the supply closet. My question is this: Is she coming on to me? And what do I do about it?

—Maurice (High on Polite and Sincere Style, Low on Playful)

Maurice, I love the fact that readers out there are screaming, "Of course, she is hitting on you, you fool!" And I have to admit that all the signs seem to be there—she is gregarious and cracking jokes, she's being playful with you and, most importantly, she keeps coming back to the place where you are. On the other hand, your reservations make sense to me, too. She seems to be this way with everyone (hugs for all) and she is volunteering for the homeless, which makes me think she has a big heart. But does that mean she's flirting with you?

The bigger clue for me is your flirting style. Guys who are high on Polite and Sincere and low on Playful (and Physical) have their "flirting switch" stuck in the off position. They do not perceive the world through a flirtatious lens. Men (and women, but men particularly) who are high on both Polite and Sincere see interactions with the opposite sex as platonic—almost by definition. They do not think anyone is flirting with them, they tend to back away from sexually charged situations and they don't act fast. In fact, if they act at all, they nearly always favor the so-called nice guy approach. This means they aren't likely to start coming on strong, even to a woman they like.

So what to do? Well, the good news is that Mary seems like a catch, and even if she is interested in only being friends right now, Sincere flirts often make friends first and then pursue romance. So I have three suggestions. First, it is likely that you feel pretty comfortable making an emotional connection, and you are already sharing with Mary something that is personally meaningful for the two of you. You need to start steering that conversation toward some personal details. Is she seeing someone? What kind of things does she like to do? Look for questions that convey to her that you are interested (because you are), but you are also trying to see if she is available. Second, chances are you aren't going to develop into Don Juan overnight. But you might be able to embrace Mary's enthusiasm by mimicking her playfulness. If you see keys hanging out of her pocket, return the favor. Give her a hug before she does to show that you like being close to her. If you don't want to come on strong, at least meet her halfway.

Finally, once you can get your mettle up, you've got to find a way to context-shift. You need to show Mary that you want to spend time with her one-on-one. This will help her see that you are ready to spend time with her alone, and get those hugs all to yourself.

Chapter Four

THE PLAYFUL STYLE

Jared, Melissa, Marco and Emma met early on a Friday night for drinks at their favorite club. It was still early and the place was pretty empty. After the first round, the four friends started swapping stories about past conquests. Melissa was giving Jared a hard time about the type of women he meets at bars.

"I saw you last week with that one girl. You know, the one who is always coming up to talk to you," Melissa said.

"I don't know what you're talking about," Jared laughed.

Melissa shot him a look. "You know, the girl with caked-on makeup. She looks a little like an orange. You went home with her, didn't you?"

"She does *not* look like that," Jared protested.

"Yeah, right. Whatever, man. I saw her, too," said Marco.

"Please!" Jared said. "You can't say she isn't hot. She may be obnoxious, but she is definitely hot. I'll admit, even though this may sound rude, that girls like her love to talk about themselves."

"Oh, *come on*," said Emma, "You are so clearly trying to change the subject."

But Melissa persisted, "So did you take her home or not?"

"No matter where I went, she always seemed to be hanging around. So last week I was drinking pretty hard and I was pretty wasted. I asked her to drive me to Taco Bell to get some food. I also made her buy my food because I said I was out of cash. Then I had her drop me off at home. She wanted to kiss me. So we did. Then, I said, 'Thanks,' and got out of the car."

"You expect me to believe that was it?" Melissa asked incredulously.

"Believe it or not, but that was *it*. The next day she called me. She wanted to make sure I had her number. She left a message, 'Just in case you need anymore Taco Bell.' It was hilarious."

"Guys think they are so smooth," said Emma. "I have a better story. Maybe a month or so ago, I was hanging out at The Well, and I happened to run into this guy that I had kinda been blowing off. Long story, but whatever. That night, it was pretty late and it started pouring. I couldn't find any of my friends to get a ride home."

"Was that the same night you texted me about a ride?" Marco asked.

"Yeah," Emma replied. "And by the way, I still hate you for that. You are *not* forgiven! Anyway, I started to flirt with that guy—the one I had blown off. I asked if he hated me; I played like I was sorry, so he offered me a ride home. The guy I blew off ended up taking me across town. Guys are such pushovers."

Jared smiled. "I'd say you are a pro."

"You two are terrible," Marco chimed in.

"Like you are any better," said Melissa. "What about that time you went up to that girl just to tell her she was dumb."

"I didn't tell her *she* was dumb," Marco objected. "I told her she was *being* dumb for talking with this other guy. He was a total loser. I was doing her a favor. I hate girls who think they're all that, like they're supermodels or something. I can't be around anyone who thinks she's better than everyone else. I like to knock girls like that down a peg. Besides I did the whole thing with a smile on my face, so she knew I was just kidding."

"Why do guys think that girls like it when a guy acts like a jerk?" complained Melissa.

"Because it works," Marco boasted. "That dumb girl totally loved it. The moment I told her she was dumb, that's when she started liking me. She gave me her number that night. Some guys don't have the personality to pull that off, so they come off as colossal jerks. But I flirt with my *winning* personality."

Emma laughed, "What do you mean, your winning personality? You *are* a total jerk around girls."

"Don't lie. You like it," Marco laughed. "Look, I can be mean to people without them even realizing I'm being mean. I used to call my ex-girlfriend ugly. She was totally gorgeous and she knew it. Sometimes she needed to be told that she was ugly. I did that for her."

"That's probably why she is your ex-girlfriend now," Jared pointed out. "But I'm with Marco on this one. Everyone knows the whole thing is a total game. Girls play the game. Guys play along, too. That's what it's all about."

"Yeah, picking on a girl's looks is the same thing as using some line. It's all part of the game," Marco agreed. "And, girls, you know you like it when guys let you know that you look good, with all that 'You are the most beautiful girl in the room' stuff. You like to know that whatever it is you are doing is working."

Melissa looked at Emma, nodded and said, "Yeah, but everybody likes compliments, not just girls. I *do* like it when guys tell me, 'I like your hair,' 'Your eyes are pretty' or 'You girls look like fun.' But so what?"

Emma agreed, "Meeting people and having fun is what it's all about. Besides, most of the time when I go out, I'm with a group of my girlfriends. Not with you two," she said, pointing to Marco and Jared with a laugh. "Last weekend Melissa and I went to The Well with some girlfriends and we had no trouble attracting the guys," she laughed.

"Ahh, how easy it is to be a woman," Jared said. "Guys have to buy the drinks, have to start the conversation and have to approach women."

"Except for the last time we were here," said Marco. "Remember that girl at another table who kept looking over at us? I pointed straight at her the next time she did that and told her 'Stop judging!' She came over with her friend to ask what was that about. She did *all* the work."

"And I guess my Taco Bell girl did all the work, too," said Jared. "Whatever, it's all in good fun."

"Well, yeah," Emma admitted. "A lot of my flirting is just for fun. It's not because I want to find a boy to go home with. Besides, I don't need a boyfriend—I have you guys."

All three nodded in agreement, and Marco got up to get them another round.

HOW TO SPOT A PLAYFUL FLIRT

1. A Playful flirt will flirt even when there is obviously no relationship potential.
2. A Playful flirt might flirt to try to get something from you.
3. A Playful flirt will joke around with you to try to get to know you better.
4. If you are at a bar, a Playful flirt might tease you a little to try to pick you up.
5. Playful flirts will initiate some sarcastic back-and-forth banter. If you like it, send it right back at them.
6. If you are in a friends-with-benefits relationship with someone, she is probably a Playful flirt (you might be the Playful flirt in this situation, too!).
7. Playful flirts will flirt with you while wearing a wedding ring (and you aren't their spouse).
8. It is pretty clear that a Playful flirt is interested in tonight, not tomorrow or forever.
9. Playful flirts will send you sexy texts when they flirt.
10. If you find out after meeting a guy that he fudged some of the facts about his past relationships on his online dating profile, he is probably a Playful flirt.

These four friends give us some pretty clear insights into the world of the Playful flirt. Marco uses some playful put-downs to meet women, Emma can get a guy she treats badly to take her home on a rainy night, Melissa isn't looking for a relationship and Jared can get a free meal from a persistent girl. Playful flirts know that flirting is a means to an end, and they have a good time getting to that end.

QUOTABLE

"I'll flirt with anyone from garbagemen to grandmothers."

—Madonna

The Playful flirt sees flirting as a game. For Playful flirts, it is fun to meet people, to chat them up and to try to get other people to fall for them, or at least like them. The Playful flirting style reflects a flippant attitude toward flirting. The Playful flirt thinks that flirting is a fun, esteem-boosting thing to do—something that shouldn't be taken too seriously. It is done for its own sake—no (romantic) ties required. Playful flirts flirt with people for the sake of flirting, even people they aren't interested in hooking up with or dating. Playful flirts are not worried about how other people may interpret their behavior because they believe everyone knows that flirting shouldn't be taken so seriously.

At heart, Playful flirts recognize that flirting is a way to feel sexy, exciting, inviting and desirable. They like to attract attention, play little games and have a good time. Compared with all the others styles, the Playful flirt understands that flirting is a powerful tool to get what you want—a free drink or special attention—or to avoid things you don't want—like a bad grade. For Playful flirts, these are little added bonuses that come along with flirting. They have absolutely no problem with using flirting to get what they want. And this isn't always done consciously. Playful flirts react to situations in a playful way. They may not always be planning the things that come along with Playful flirting; they just behave in a way that makes others want to play along.

WHO IS A PLAYFUL FLIRT?

Both Men and Women

The Playful flirting style is equally distributed among both men and women. When it comes to the singles scene, men and women both benefit by developing a Playful style because so much of it is inherently fun. But Playful flirts see flirting as something to do at a bar, or with waiters and waitresses, cops, teachers and anyone else they think they can charm with their Playful style. That is, they know flirting can be used to get something—even if it is just attention from the opposite sex.

RESEARCH SAYS

Men and women are equally motivated to flirt to get something (like a free drink) and to boost their self-esteem.

25–35-Year-Olds

You could call this the decade of Playful flirting. The late 20s to early 30s are basically *the time* for flirting for fun. This may be because of what you can get away with at that age—it's easier for a younger person to flirt casually and tease playfully. This behavior may be considered awkward or unseemly in someone 35 or older. Playfulness generally seems to be reserved for people who are young enough to pull it off. It could also be highest at this time in life because 25-35-year-olds are likely out of school, independent and hanging out in their own little urban tribe. People that age believe they still have time to figure out what committed relationships are all about.

Physical and Not Very Polite

As discussed in the Physical flirting chapter, the connection between the Playful and Physical flirting styles is pretty strong. Playful flirts are comfortable expressing their physical interest, but, as we shall see, that doesn't mean they actually *mean anything* by it. Unlike the Physical style, which leads to some pretty intense experiences of physical attraction and romantic chemistry, the Playful flirt doesn't feel flirting is about romance. Playful flirts might pretend they feel that way, but there is a good chance they are faking it. This would be like when a guy says to a girl he barely knows, "Girl, you know you are totally gorgeous and I can't get over you." The Playful flirt clearly doesn't mean it. He's just being a player.

The Playful flirt is not very Polite, either. The Playful flirt thinks all the hand-wringing anxieties of the Polite flirt are nonsense. This is especially true for female Playful flirts. Women are characteristically more Polite than men, and men are characteristically more, to borrow some British terminology, caddish with the birds. As a result, women who adopt a more Playful style are particularly impolite flirts. They are less likely to adhere to norms of politeness and social grace. As you might guess, this also means that women who are Playful flirts are not very Traditional. They are not very ladylike. For men, this Playful but not Traditional link just isn't there. A Traditional man can be Playful, if he wants. Think of the guy who is all buttons and collars and proper manners at his job, but he also likes to tease and pick on the younger women around the office. He can be Playful and Traditional, too.

THE SURVEY SAYS

Playful women are much more likely to say, "I don't think it makes a difference who makes the first move. I think if you're interested in a guy, you should pursue him."

Rebellious, Haphazard and Cool

The story of the four Playful friends at the opening of this chapter shows that you have to be a rule breaker to be a Playful flirt. Playful flirts tend to adopt a devil-may-care attitude about almost everything. You generally have to believe that getting your way is more important than making other people happy or avoiding hurting their feelings. If someone's ego gets bruised or his feelings are hurt, the Playful flirt would defend herself by saying, "Well, that just goes with the territory. It is really your fault for taking it so seriously." Just as Marco said, the Playful flirt thinks that sometimes people need to be put in their place, even at the cost of hurt feelings.

At the same time, Playful flirts are quite socially adept. They are able to put on a good social performance and can act a part, if they need to. Playful flirts can change the way they act or how they do things if it gives them some social advantage. If all this sounds like the classic John Malkovich and Glenn Close drama *Dangerous Liaisons,* you are getting the right idea. Love is a game that Playful flirts can play successfully to their advantage. But to play this game, you can't be too concerned with other people or their feelings. Niceness is for suckers, when it comes to the game of love as played by the Playful flirt.

CYBER-FLIRTING

A woman with a Playful style might shoot you a sexy text message just for fun.

WHERE THE PLAYFUL FLIRT FINDS LOVE

The Playful flirt is hard to pin down when it comes to having a home field advantage. The tricky thing about Playful flirts is that they like being at bars and clubs and they like being single. So much so that they don't really care about trying to meet people. When they do meet people, it certainly isn't for the purpose of forming a meaningful relationship or seeking a committed partner. As a consequence, their home turf is being used for a different game entirely. They aren't looking to find a boyfriend or girlfriend, a husband or wife. They are there to have fun.

Consider the following:

- **The Playful flirt** loves being single.
- **The Playful flirt** likes to go dancing and to dance seductively, maybe to even put on a little show to see what kind of attention it brings.
- **The Playful flirt** likes going to bars to meet people, but is not there to try to form any type of relationship—either a hookup or a long-term romance.
- **Playful flirts** don't approach people at bars—not even someone they consider attractive.
- **Playful flirts** think they are better than their friends at flirting, and they think their friends are really good at it, too.

Taking all that in, what is the real story? Playful flirts have the ability to hook up with someone they meet, but they don't really want to use it. They like to go out dancing and get attention, but they don't go out of their way to try to pick up strangers. To get into the mind of the Playful flirt, you have to remember that, for them, flirting is done nearly exclusively for its own sake, or for the perks it brings. Flirting makes the Playful flirt feel good. It has nearly nothing to do with romance.

In the eHarmony Survey, we asked how it *feels* to flirt. Playful flirts were off the charts when it came to this answer: Flirting makes me feel attractive! Interestingly, flirting was also their way of feeling closer to people. This means that flirting helps Playful flirts feel a sense of connection with someone. But the second half of our question really drove home the point. We asked whether or not it felt good if someone flirted back, and Playful flirts responded with an overwhelming, Meh? Or I don't know, sort of, I guess. That is, they don't care that much if someone flirts back with them. They want to flirt because of what it does for them, but they aren't looking to flirt because of what it does for someone else. They don't want to spend time trying to figure out what other people are trying to communicate when they flirt. It is the buzz they feel when flirting that makes them feel good, not the buzz they get from others being attracted to them.

THE SURVEY SAYS

The Playful flirt is the only one of the five flirting styles who said "No" when asked, "Do you communicate your romantic interest when you flirt?"

THE PLAYFUL TACTIC

Playful Men Use the Neg

The term *neg* became part of everyday talk about flirting thanks to the *Mystery Method* and VH1's *The Pickup Artist,* and there are lots of good examples of guys using negs on women from the reality show. But the best one was in the movie *Crazy Stupid Love.* The ultradreamy Ryan Gosling plays a self-created pickup artist named Jacob. He decides to initiate the recently dumped Cal, played by Steve Carell, into his pickup artist dojo and teach his protégé the ways of love. In one scene in the movie, Jacob is talking to a beautiful woman as Cal looks on. After she starts talking about her family, Jacob interrupts and tells her it is bor-ing…at least for his purposes. Because, Jacob says, he has a bet with Cal that she is entirely too gorgeous to be interesting. This is a perfectly executed neg. It pays a compliment while at the same time forcing a woman to defend herself. She has to explain or show how she is interesting if she really wants the compliment. The attention Jacob is giving her is contingent on her impressing him. So why does this work?

As you might have guessed, men who are Playful flirts do this all the time. Like Marco's strategy of telling beautiful women they are ugly or dumb, the Playful flirt thinks it is all in good fun. A graduate student at the University of Kansas named Melanie Canterberry and I took on these very questions about negs in a study looking at a set of aggressive pickup strategies. We found that *by far* the Playful flirting style was the style most strongly associated with men who tease women. Men who are Playful flirts aren't overly persistent or pushy with women—they can take it or leave it—so they aren't that competitive. They aren't trying to get a girl alone or take her home. But they constantly tease women because it is fun for them.

Playful Ladies Love to be Teased

Now the real shocker, at least for Melanie and me, was that women who are Playful flirts like it when men use aggressive pickup strategies across the board. Women who are Playful flirts like it when men are competitive and try to outfox or outmaneuver other guys. They like it when men try to get them alone and get them in bed. These girls love cheesy pickup lines. They think the teasing is adorable and inviting. From the point of view of the Playful girl, it is all in good fun. Playful guys are content to pull a Jacob from *Crazy Stupid Love* and simply tease and neg a woman for the fun of it. But the Playful ladies like it when guys take it to another level. They enjoy it when men are teasing *and* competing *and* being persistent throughout the night. For the Playful ladies, it is pleasurable to have that kind of attention.

So there you have it, good evidence that Playful men and women are made for each other. This explains why men's teasing tactics work so well. The men and women out there who share a Playful flirting style speak the same flirting language. They get a kick out of playing little games and they both agree that it is all in good fun. As long as one Playful flirt finds another Playful flirt, it probably doesn't end all too badly. Neither person is in it for a long-term, committed relationship. No one is confused about what it is all about. Now, when the Playful flirt uses those tactics with another flirting style, it will end badly. Hurt feelings, broken hearts, confusion and outright drama are all likely consequences. Good thing that Emma Stone's character in *Crazy Stupid Love* avoided Jacob when he first tried to pick her up. It makes for a much better story that way.

CYBER-FLIRTING

Because she thinks you like her and want to meet her, a Playful woman can really get into online chatting.

SEX AND THE CASUAL FLING

The Playful flirt tends to have casual attitudes about sex, too. You can probably imagine why. If flirting is no big deal, it would make sense that sex isn't a big deal, either. My research provides some solid evidence that this is exactly the case for the Playful flirt. In the FSI Survey, I found that Playful flirts believe that sex without love is totally fine. They don't have a problem getting into a purely physical relationship without the rules and restrictions of a committed relationship. They don't judge other people who sleep around, either. However, there were some key differences when comparing Playful men and Playful women.

Women who are Playful flirts seem to act on these sexually permissive attitudes a bit more than men do. Playful women were more likely than Playful men to have one-night stands. Also, women who were more Playful flirts had more sexual desire than men who were Playful flirts. Playful women liked to consider what kind of sexual possibilities might arise when meeting a new guy. Although Playful flirts in general are open to no-strings-attached sex, women who are Playful flirts are more likely to have done it and are more likely to want to do it again than are men.

The bottom line: a Playful flirting style tells you more about a woman's sexual past and her sexual future than it does for a man.

THE SURVEY SAYS

Playful flirts don't think that meeting in bars precludes them from developing a long-term romance.

Casual, Not Committed

Just for a moment, let's consider what would happen if a Playful flirt just happened to stumble into a committed relationship. What is that experience like for her? One way a Playful flirt might start a relationship is through a night of casual sex turning into something more. My research shows that the Playful flirt isn't as well suited to a committed relationship as other flirting styles are. In the eHarmony Survey, we asked people what their most recent romantic relationship was like, and the Playful flirt was fairly noncommittal across the board. By a long shot, the Playful flirt was the most likely to describe her last romantic relation-ship as a casual fling. In fact, nearly *half* of those who said their last relationship was a fling were Playful flirts. When describing their last relationship, Playful flirts had a weak emotional *and* a weak physical connection with their last boyfriend or girlfriend. They were not terribly attracted to their last boyfriend or girl-friend all that much, either. Being a Playful flirt was not related to feeling particularly physically or sexually attracted to the individual's last partner. So why were they in that relationship to begin with? The only good thing that a Playful flirt could say about her last relationship was that she had fun! Hey, at least it was good while it lasted.

THE SURVEY SAYS

Playful flirts are 13 percent more likely to use sex to try to start a long-term relationship.

Playing the Part of Player

This cavalier attitude about flirting and sex also translates into the Playful flirt's feelings about love. Research tells us that there are six types of love. The one and *only* type of love that is related to the Playful flirting style is called *ludic,* or game players. Like a lone wolf out on the mountainside, the ludic lover tends to like to play games, keep secrets and go behind his lover's back to keep things interesting. Ludic lovers keep their romantic lives as uncommitted as possible. They do not try to get very close or intimate with their partners throughout the duration of the relationship. To keep the game going and the sense of excitement and newness alive, they don't like to share their personal thoughts and feelings. The ludic lover also sees sex as something done for pleasure, not for intimacy.

Given this player mentality, what other sorts of games might the Playful flirt engage in? In the FSI Survey, I found out some startling statistics. Playful flirts were 38 percent more likely than other flirting styles to flirt with other people while in a committed relationship, and were 17 percent more likely to date more than one person at once. Talk about needing to keep secrets!

THE SURVEY SAYS

Playful flirts are 15 percent more likely to lie to get someone interested in them.

This game-playing attitude toward love, the persistent flirting while in a relationship and the multiple dating partners all go together. These things are all about the hookup pathway to romance and a hookup disposition in general. In an extensive study of hooking up on college campuses, Elizabeth Paul and her colleagues found that students with a ludic love style were hooking up quite a bit—easily in excess of once every two weeks. And many, but not all, of these hookups included some fooling around or sexual contact with someone they never saw again. It all makes sense. You can't expect Playful flirts to pass up on the opportunity to hook up when they are so good at playing the game.

Flirting or friendly?

All this points a pretty rough picture for Playful flirts who come to the conclusion that they want something more romantic. Moving past having multiple hookup partners to having a steady boyfriend or girlfriend is tough for the Playful flirt. What happens if and when a Playful flirt tries to transition into a more serious relationship?

The first thing to keep in mind is that Playful flirts are not just effective in a bar or club. They use their flirting style to their advantage nearly all the time. In fact, Playful flirts are more likely than any other flirting style to have the experience that people think they are flirting even when they aren't. This happens when they are actually *trying* to be friendly. It seems that they just have a flirtatious disposition. This makes a lot of sense if you remember that, for the Playful flirt, making a connection with people through flirting feels good. They just can't turn off these good feelings so easily. I had a friend who was a Playful flirt and he told me that he felt as if flirting were a way of just showing someone attention—in a good way. When he paid attention to a lady by flirting, he felt good and he thought it made her feel good, too—sexier, more interesting, and maybe a little frisky.

Flirting and being friendly are totally tangled up for the Playful flirt. In the eHarmony Survey, we asked whether or not Playful flirts had this experience: they tried to seriously flirt with someone, but it was misinterpreted as being friendly. Interestingly, this happens to Playful flirts all the time. If you have a good friend who is a highly Playful flirt, it is probably a good idea to realize she doesn't mean much by flirting. If you see someone who is always flirtatious with everyone around her—a person who uses flirting to get her way—and she starts flirting with you, it would probably be best to doubt it was sincere. It would be safer for you to think of it as friendly. But because the Playful flirt is known for being flirtatious like this, it can be hard for the Playful flirt to flirt with romantic intent when she wants to.

Unlike Polite flirts, Playful flirts don't typically flirt with people they know very well and they don't use friendship as a way to start a romantic relationship. They are interested in lots of people, and they flirt with lots of people, but they don't tend to seek out romance through friendship. So where do they find love?

The Workplace

The good news for Playful flirts is that there is one place that might give them a slight advantage: the workplace. Although it is taboo to flirt at work, especially between superiors and subordinates, work is one of the most common places for people to meet their future husband or wife. In the FSI Survey, I found that Playful flirts were 12 percent more likely to have met their last serious relationship partner at work. This is because the work environment gives the Playful flirt several advantages. To start with, Playful flirts are willing to break some rules, so workplace taboos won't inhibit them. Because they are always coming off as flirtatious, they have the advantage of putting themselves out there in a relatively low relationship-seeking environment. Essentially, they stand apart as being more flirtatious than other, more restrained employees.

THE SURVEY SAYS

Nearly 16 percent of the 4,500 people surveyed met their most recent romantic partner at work.

RELATIONSHIPS AND LOVE

When I am interviewed, I am often asked which flirting style is the best. I always answer that it depends on what you want. The Playful flirting style is a perfect example of this. Playful flirts may be naturally flirtatious, but when they decide they actually want to meet someone or get close to him, their approach gets misinterpreted. People around Playful flirts can't seem to figure out whether they are flirting to get another boost to their self-esteem or they're flirting with more serious romantic intent. Their regular, everyday behavior looks so much like flirting that they can't get any other message across. They are so naturally flirtatious that it is hard for them to find a pathway to start a meaningful relationship.

> ### RESEARCH SAYS
>
> Once in a relationship, people tend to stop prowling the hookup scene.

Playful Flirts in Love

Of the four Playful friends introduced at the beginning of the chapter, two ended up together. Melissa gave Jared such a hard time about the women he met because she was always trying to figure out what those girls had that she didn't have. Melissa had been interested in Jared for a while, but nothing ever seemed to happen between the two of them. Jared liked Melissa, too. For her sake, he always held back a little with women at bars and clubs, especially when he was out with Melissa. The two of them just couldn't figure out how to make it work. That is, until one cold night.

> ### RESEARCH SAYS
>
> Women who like to date Playful and flirty guys are looking to have fun on that date, but they are also open to the possibility of an exclusive relationship.

It was a cold, cold Friday night. Jared and Melissa were out on the town, as usual. They had had some drinks together and neither had met anyone interesting. As they shared a cab ride home, Melissa asked Jared, "Do you want to come inside? We could get some Taco Bell."

Jared laughed and said, "I wouldn't mind eating something with you. But, please, no more Taco Bell!"

That night, one thing led to another and they hooked up. Jared began putting his clothes back on to go home, as he always did with women. One of his rules for himself was he never slept over. Melissa looked at the window and said, "It's snowing outside. You could stay if you wanted." Jared looked back at Melissa and knew that she was serious. This wasn't just a line or a game. He stayed the night and long into the next day.

That snow day marked the beginning of their relationship. You could say they were friends with benefits before that point, but neither were ready before that snowy night to take it to the next level. After that night, they started hanging out more and it very gradually became more serious. Neither wanted to talk about it. Neither wanted to have any expectations for their relationship. Neither wanted the fun, casual thing they had together to come to an end.

Soon afterward, rather than going to the clubs, Melissa and Jared decided to stay in. One night they went to Jared's place for a change. While watching a movie together on the couch, Jared said to Melissa, "Is this us? Are we a thing now?" Melissa thought about it and without looking away from the TV, said, "Yeah, I guess we are." Then, she smiled to herself and snuggled into Jared to get a little more comfortable.

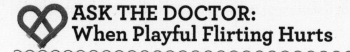

ASK THE DOCTOR:
When Playful Flirting Hurts

Dear Dr. Hall,

My husband has a hurtful habit of flagrantly flirting with young waitresses. It makes me feel bad, especially when he does this in front of our kids. I know he loves me. Why is he doing this?

—Anonymous

For most people, flirting is romantic, novel and unpredictable, which is exciting and inviting. But flirting can also be hurtful when someone you love or your partner is flirting with someone else. The good news is that your husband isn't necessarily flirting to be mean-spirited.

My first take on this situation is cut-and-dried: your husband is a classic Playful flirt. Playful flirts see flirting as harmless fun. They don't think that flirting has anything to do with seeking a relationship, but often flirt for a boost of self-esteem or because they want to get something out of the exchange. If your husband is flirtatious with lots of people, not just young waitresses, and if he was a Playful flirt when you two first started dating, then you have a Playful flirt on your hands. If you ask Playful flirts why they flirt, they'll likely say, "I didn't mean anything by it." And that is true *for them.*

However, you are being hurt by his actions and I expect that you are worried about two important things: (1) It makes you look bad in front of your family, and (2) you're concerned about what it might mean to your relationship.

First things first: I actually think that your husband's flirting while you and the kids are around is not a danger sign. The conventional wisdom is that people who are in relationships flirt because they are unhappy, and there is some research to support this. However, I believe that if he is flirting with you and the kids present, it has little to do with how happy he is with you—it's more likely just in his nature to flirt that way. This doesn't excuse his behavior, but it gives you a way of understanding it.

And the waitress is probably flirting back with him to get a better tip. Research says that when a female waitress lightly touches a male patron's hand or shoulder, it increases her tip significantly. In fact, if your kids are right there, the waitress is on particularly safe ground. Unlike a creepy guy by himself or a guy on the prowl with a group of friends, a family man is unlikely to cause trouble or make her work life uncomfortable. All this points to a harmless exchange from your husband's and from the waitress's point of view.

But from your point of view, this is simply unacceptable. His style of flirting may be something he views as harmless and fun, but you need to let him know that while you understand that he doesn't mean anything by it, his behavior upsets you.

Chapter Five

THE SINCERE STYLE

ANDREW

The last time I went out? Well, that's a tough one. I don't go out much. When I do go out, I am in no rush. I like to hang out for a few hours with my friends before we head out the door. If you are asking about the last time I went out to a bar, the last time I remember was Halloween. That night I went to a bar with a bunch of friends. We just had some drinks and had a good time. I went home by myself and went to bed. I know it isn't much, but that was a good time for me.

I don't approach women. Well, maybe I do. But not in the way guys usually do. You see, I'm about as smooth as sandpaper. Now my friend Brad, he is the man. He knows how to flirt with girls. He is persistent and clever. I watch what he does and,

I don't know, I'm just not feeling it. It seems like a lot of work to put on the charm. Brad isn't really interested in making friends and sometimes he can make girls a little, well, uncomfortable. But, damn, if he isn't good at it. Maybe it's worth it for him, but for me, I'm not so sure.

Look, I'm a nice guy. At least that's what girls tell me. I think my looks are part of what makes girls interested—that is, if they *are* interested. I have an innocent face and a nice smile. Girls mainly like me because I try to get to know them. The thing is, I won't go up and talk to a girl unless I am interested already. I will watch her for a while and get a sense of what she is like. You can just tell by looking. When I talk to her, I want to know better what she is really like, what she is all about. But once I get going, I can be a real talker and a good listener, too. I want to know more about her than what she is drinking and what parties she has been to. I like to get to know who she really is, you know? I feel as if I have a lot to say and share, and I'm looking for that in another person.

I just don't flirt very often. I tried once to flirt with a girl who was a friend of mine. I did it kind of as a joke. But, she wasn't having it. You could say I bombed. And a year ago, I was at a bar and I tried to pick up on this cheerleader-type girl. You know—blond, bubbly and dressed to impress. She seemed bored. She kept looking over her shoulder to see if there was someone more interesting to talk to. Maybe she was looking to get a drink from some other guy. Since then I've steered away from that kind of girl.

When I'm around people, I want to make a real connection. When I meet a girl, I want to become friends with her rather than hook up with her. It's not that I don't ever want to hook up or that I don't want to take a girl home—although that has never happened to me. It's just that it isn't what I'm there for. I'm there to hang out with my friends and have a good time. If I talk to a girl, I don't try to game her or impress her or put a move on her. Flirting for me is just an easy way to talk to somebody. If someone is easy to talk to, it's like you are flirting with her already.

JULIA

I don't go out much because I work a lot. When I do go, I'm there to have fun. I'm never the person hanging in the corner. I'm outgoing, and I like to meet people. But, I usually hang back to see if a guy will approach me. I don't put myself out there enough to have the chance to be rejected.

With guys it's pretty cut-and-dried, isn't it? If he's interested, he will buy me a drink. When a guy asks me if I want a drink, I tell him, "Let's do a shot together." I like to do shots. I think that is the best icebreaker around. It instantly makes you part of the group. Have a shot and you are part of the party.

I *hate* boring bar talk. What do you do? Where did you go to school? Ugh. I don't like chitchat and I really don't want to talk about major life events. I came here to have a good time, and I'm talking to you, dummy, so obviously I am available. I also have a secret strategy about how to talk with guys. You know the best way? Talk about sports. I'd say that is the number one thing I talk to guys about. I feel comfortable, too, because I pay attention to the big names and teams. And guys can work with that.

This guy I met the other weekend was really cute and I got him talking about football for like 30 minutes. He thought he had hit the jackpot with me. Afterward, I gave him my number. Sports are perfect for that because no one confuses talking about the playoffs with some sort of deep conversation.

I can usually tell when a guy is truly interested in me and when he is just being nice. I'm outgoing enough, and I can usually keep a conversation going. Maybe we're getting along well enough, but I'd say if he's talking to everyone the same way he is talking to me, I'd assume he's just a nice guy. Especially if he's talking to my girlfriends like that, too. If he is trying to sit closer to me or trying to fit in some touching—like resting his hand on my hip or leaning in closer to me—then he's interested. I can't really tell whether he is all that interested by what he is saying—it's what he does that counts.

I'm also pretty sarcastic around guys. I like it when guys are not very serious, either. People shouldn't take flirting so seriously. I hate it when people think it means something or that it is all romantic or something. Flirting gets a bad rap because people think they have to be either coming on to you or having some deep conversation. Let's not get overly close at a bar, OK?

HOW TO SPOT A SINCERE FLIRT

1. When getting to know you, a Sincere flirt will ask a lot of questions and will later remember important details about you, even before asking you out on a date.

2. A Sincere flirt is going to be really open and share a lot of personal stuff with you while getting to know you, particularly a Sincere guy. If you find yourself on the receiving end of his attention, this is a sign that he is interested in getting closer to you.

3. If you are chatting online, a Sincere flirt is going to keep it very positive and friendly.

4. A Sincere flirt might complain about the loud music at the club making it hard to have a good conversation with you.

5. Sincere flirts will share interesting ideas or experiences they have had, whether the context suits the conversation or not. If you share their passion for ideas, let them know—they think intellect is a sexy quality!

6. When on a date, the Sincere flirt will attentively try to figure out whether you two share interests and hobbies.

7. Sincere flirts are kind and warm people, so much so that they might forget to let you know you look good and they are interested in something more physical. Don't take their sweetness as a sign of a lack of attraction.

8. Sincere flirts really like being flirted with. They find it flattering and appreciate the attention. But do expect a bit of embarrassment or shyness after you compliment them.

9. Don't be surprised if Sincere flirts don't seem as if they are picking up on your signs or aren't interested in something more than friendship. A Sincere flirt

doesn't pay attention to or attempt to communicate physical attraction clearly.

10. Sincere flirts are unwilling to change their point of view just for the sake of agreement, so they may seem as if they have strong beliefs.

It is probably pretty easy to guess that Andrew is the Sincere flirt and Julia is quite the opposite. Andrew scores high on the Sincere style and Julia scores low. The reason I presented you with both sides of the Sincere style is that both the Andrews and the Julias out there tell us something about what the Sincere style is and what it isn't. For every flirting style, you could be high or low. And just because you are one style, say, Physical, doesn't mean you are necessarily high or low on Sincere. The question then becomes, What did Andrew and Julia say that let you know what flirting means to them?

A dictionary definition of *sincere* is "free of deceit or falseness; earnest; genuine; real." But *flirting* is defined as "to act amorously without serious intention." So isn't the Sincere flirting style an oxymoron? *No way!* At least not in my book. The Sincere style includes some of the most important aspects of flirting. The whole idea that flirting can't have sincere intent behind it is just plain ridiculous.

All of us can think of an occasion where we felt that someone we just met was truly and genuinely interested in us. Not just by what he did, but by what he said and how he listened. And it probably felt really good to be there, soaking up that sincerity. The Sincere style is marked by this authenticity.

The Sincere flirt makes a connection by showing sincere and personal interest in someone else. For the Sincere flirt, forging an emotional bond with a potential romantic partner *is* flirting. It is like what Andrew said, "Flirting for me is just an easy way to talk to somebody." When you discover a connection with someone through sharing yourself, it creates a little buzz inside you. This buzz through self-disclosure is the very nature of flirting for people like Andrew. For people like Julia, talking about personal stuff is uncomfortable and unwelcome. The Sincere flirt knows that one of the primary ways to get close to someone is to share yourself and get the other person talking about herself, too. The Sincere flirting style communicates romantic or sexual interest through paying sincere attention to a potential partner's experiences, hopes, dreams and passions. For this style of flirting, sexual chemistry develops *through* communication and self-disclosure. You could say that, for the Sincere flirt having a good conversation *is* flirting.

RESEARCH SAYS

When you share information about yourself with a stranger, you feel closer to her. When you feel that this new person likes what you have to say, you will share even more.

People who are very low on the Sincere style, like Julia, find that whole process pretty boring. They would like to keep it light and fun. Both Andrew and Julia enjoyed hanging out with their friends. They both liked to be at a bar to have fun and not necessarily to pick up strangers. When the occasion presented itself, both Andrew and Julia were up for meeting someone new. The big difference is how they saw words and stories as being part of getting to know someone. Andrew liked getting to know people on a deeper level and Julia believed it was a waste of time. A Sincere style of flirting can be painfully slow for someone who doesn't like all the *talking* it requires. Because it is generally nonthreatening and nonsexual, the Sincere style is a bad fit for someone who likes a little danger and mystery. Or someone who likes sarcastic and teasing banter. The Sincere style just isn't everyone's thing.

WHO IS A SINCERE FLIRT?

The Most Common Style

Women tend to have a more developed Sincere style of flirting than men do. Women tend to like men who approach them using more emotional connection and self-disclosure—they find it attractive. But the Sincere style is the most common flirting style for everyone. Past research has shown that emotional disclosure is the most effective, most agreeable and least phony way to get someone to like you. This matches up nicely with the results of both of our studies. Far and away, the Sincere style was the highest-scoring flirting style in the eHarmony and the FSI Surveys. No other flirting style even came close. Most of us are at least a little bit Sincere when it comes right down to it.

THE SURVEY SAYS

When flirting, 40 percent of women and 30 percent of men think that sharing common interests is a sexy quality.

All Ages

For some flirting styles, people change the way they communicate romantic interest as they age (see the Traditional style for a good example). But people of all ages are equally likely to be Sincere flirts. This is probably because people understand at a pretty basic level that the communication of romantic attraction in a sincere and heartfelt way is appealing and desirable. Who we are inside is best revealed through the process of sharing. If you communicate romance by getting to know the real person behind what he looks like, the Sincere style will suit you over your whole lifetime—even as people's looks, interests and perspectives change.

Complementary Styles

Let start by what the Sincere style *isn't* related to. The Sincere flirting style has no connection with the Traditional and Playful styles. It's a different story for the Polite and Physical styles.

Sincere flirts are comfortable communicating their physical attraction physically and nonverbally but also tend to avoid the direct approach and can find aggressive strangers to be unappealing. Now how is this possible? The Sincere style is the communication of emotional and personal interest in another person, not the communication of sexual interest, per se. As in Andrew's story, he was sexually attracted to women, but he found that having a good conversation with them was the best way to show his desire and elicit sexual desire in women (however effective that may be in reality). He didn't like creeps who were aggressive with girls. That is why he knew that his friend's style wouldn't work for him. Andrew was a gentleman, rather than persistent, direct or pushy. In short, he was a more Polite flirt. The bottom line is this: Sincere flirts don't approach aggressively, but once they find an interesting person to talk to, they can use their physicality to get the message across if they need to. Connection first, sex later, but in either case keep it ladylike or gentlemanly.

RESEARCH SAYS

According to studies using brain-scanning technologies, for some guys an emotional connection is as powerful and rewarding as physical connection.

Artistic, Creative, Nice and Friendly

By looking at the personality profile of each of the flirting styles, there was something very interesting about the Sincere style. I knew that Sincere types like to have deep conversations *and* that they consider themselves to be interesting people. Well, this detail ended up reflecting a very important part of their overall personality. Sincere flirts are very open to new experiences.

They tend to be artistic, creative and world travelers. They like to see and experience new things. If given the chance, they'll do something new for its own sake. No wonder they were more likely to want to have a deep conversation—they have done some seriously cool stuff. In a study I did on online dating with some colleagues, we found that people who were open to new experiences were much more honest in their online dating profiles. Why make something up if you already have an interesting life and cool things to talk about? The same goes for the Sincere flirt.

Sincere flirts are also nice. We all know that nice guys finish last (more on that little myth later), but it is also no secret that being warm, friendly, pleasant and considerate are extremely desirable qualities in a potential partner, especially someone you'd like to be with for a long time. Like Andrew, Sincere flirts are, by all standards, pretty nice people. They like to talk to other people and are outgoing, rather than introverted. They may not command a room as Physical flirts do, but Sincere flirts don't hide in a corner, either. They know how to talk and they have some important things to share. Although they could put on a good show for other people, they'd prefer to just be themselves. They don't want to change who they are to suit other people or other contexts, even though they could. Sounds pretty sincere, doesn't it?

Cyber-flirting

Sincere flirts will express a lot of positivity when chatting online; they will keep the negative stuff out of the picture.

WHERE THE SINCERE FLIRT FINDS LOVE

If you are a highly Sincere flirt and home field advantage is what you want, where should you go to play the game of love? Well, we can start by saying where you don't want go: bars and clubs. The FSI Survey revealed that people high on the Sincere style were 20 percent less likely to meet their last romantic partner in a bar or club. Instead, they relied on school, work and friends to find a new partner. There was one place that Sincere flirts started their relationship more than any other flirting style—the internet. Sincere flirts were 26 percent more likely to meet their last romantic partner online. Even though only 14 percent of people in the FSI Survey had met their partners on the internet, a lot of them were very high on the Sincere style.

CYBER-FLIRTING

Sincere flirts are really good at online flirting. When they use IM, they can get their partner to like them by establishing trust, which is a tough thing to do online.

Why are sincerity and online dating a good fit? Because of how the whole process works. If you use the internet to help you find someone, you can either match yourself or you can let a computer match you. But, either way, you start by learning about someone in a pretty static state—an online profile. Once you are matched, you might exchange a few messages, typically through an online server or through email. If that works out, then you meet in person for a drink, for dinner or maybe just for coffee to keep expectations low. (Although there are internet dating sites you can use to find a person open to short-term sex, they function quite differently than the most prominent, popular and profitable sites.) Notice, though, that the big internet dating sites direct you exclusively to only one of our three pathways—the First Date route. While there are certainly a few Hookups, there isn't a Known Quantity pathway available to you online. The good news for the Sincere style is that the First Date domain is where they really shine.

THE SINCERE FLIRT AND THE FIRST DATE

The first date is the leap from platonic to romantic. It is a turning point where things might escalate or fall off the cliff. For someone you already know through work or school or through friends, the first date is the classic context shift. By getting to know someone in a context different than the one in which you met him, you raise the stakes. This phenomenon isn't unique to dating. It also works with acquaintances we'd like to become better friends with. If we ask new friends to our home to hang out and watch basketball or reality TV or have them over for dinner, we are developing friendships. We shift contexts to get to know them better. With a crush you know from work, taking her out after work for a drink is another common context shift. Context shifts are a great way to deliver this message: I'm ready to escalate. Whatever the relationship, you are sending the message that you want to take it up a notch.

Once you are actually on a date, what are you doing there? You probably don't need research on this topic to tell you that learning about another person, becoming closer to him and having fun are the most common reasons for going on a first date. Down the list quite a bit is the possibility of sex. Think about these things in relation to what Sincere flirts do. They want closeness, they want to learn about you, they want to share and *then* they'd like to have sex. The very fact that they decided to go out on a date, rather than, say, to a keg party, means that intimacy escalation is on the agenda. Sincere flirts convey romantic interest in a way that is exactly the purpose of a first date. No wonder they look for romantic partners through internet dating. They want to get to the first date as fast as possible because it *is* their home field.

Cyber-flirting

The Sincere flirting style translates to sincerity during online dating. Sincere flirts are unwilling to misrepresent who they are, what they like to do, what kind of relationship they want and their background compared to less Sincere flirts.

GREAT PERSONALITIES GIVE YOU GREAT LOOKS

Taking this First-Date-First strategy might be a big boost for the Sincere flirt. In the film *As Good As It Gets*, Carol, played by

Helen Hunt, says to Melvin, an incredible jerk played by Jack Nicholson, "When you first entered the restaurant, I thought you were handsome...and then, of course, you spoke." The good news for people who do not have foot-in-mouth disease, like Melvin, is that it works the other way, too.

Communication theorist Dr. Kelly Albada and her colleagues argued that a person's physical attractiveness fundamentally *changes* based on what they say. We all have known for a long time that people like Melvin can ruin their good looks by being obnoxious, but people have always been somewhat suspicious that being a nice guy or girl doesn't win you any bonus points for your looks. We think that it is actually code for being unattractive, as in, "She has a nice personality." Dr. Albada found quite the opposite.

It turns out that after talking to someone we once considered average-looking and realizing they have intelligence, charisma and a good sense of humor, or are a good conversationalist, we will view them as more attractive. Check out these quotes from Dr. Albada's study: "He always had something to say"; "She said the right thing"; "He was always sincere and open." What is truly remarkable about this study is this: it is not that a person's attractive personality makes a potential partner overlook her ordinary looks. It is that a person actually *becomes* better-looking by having an outstanding personality. It is transformative. A follow-up study conducted by three different researchers found very similar results: people who were just considered average on attractiveness were given a second look when their good personality was revealed.

Research Says

A man's physical attractiveness is more malleable than a woman's attractiveness. A guy with a great personality can really improve his looks, even more than a personable woman can.

THE SINCERE FLIRT AND ATTRACTION

Now what does this have to do with the Sincere flirting style? Well, we know that Sincere flirts are also open to cool new artistic and worldly experiences and, as an added bonus, they are quite warm and kind people, too. These personality characteristics go far toward giving the impression they are great catches.

Even more important, from the perspective of the Sincere flirt, physical attraction is a process of getting to know someone. In the eHarmony Survey, we found that the Sincere style and *only* the Sincere style agreed with the statement: I find that the more I get to know people the more physically attracted I am to them. This response basically proves Dr. Albada's theory. Another thing unique to the Sincere style is agreement with this statement: Being passionate about ideas is a sexy quality. If you ask Sincere flirts what they think is a good sign of successful flirting, they will rate, "I came across as intelligent" very highly. Looking their best means revealing their best personal qualities.

Taken together, what this means is that talking, sharing, telling stories and caring about ideas, hobbies or experiences is considered flirtatious, seductive and sexy to a Sincere flirt. A couple of years back, I saw a TV advertisement that had an attractive couple holed up in their modern apartment. They spent the day lazing around in bed in their underwear reading the *New York Times* Sunday edition. Sex + reading = yummy. I'd peg them as a couple of Sincere flirts if ever there were any.

Research Says

Showing warmth, openness and emotional involvement not only creates intimacy, it is particularly attractive to people who seek intimacy, too.

THE SINGLES SCENE

The FSI Survey provided some key insights into what Sincere flirts think about the singles scene. The answer: they hate it. Sincere flirts told me they don't enjoy going to bars to meet people, they don't think it is any fun and they feel uncomfortable there. What's their problem with the local watering hole?

Well, there are several reasons Sincere flirts gave for not wanting to be part of the singles scene. The first is that they don't like being single. Let's be honest: people who like the singles scene know how to be single and know how to play the field. However, the Sincere flirt can truthfully say, "I don't like being single and I don't want to play along."

The second reason they hate the singles scene is that they don't like what the singles scene is all about. Like Andrew, Sincere flirts don't have to be dragged out like some other flirting styles (I'm looking at you, Polite style!). Once they get there, they won't be the ones hiding in a corner, either. They actually like hanging out with people quite a bit. But they just prefer to do so with their friends, and preferably at home or some other relaxed place. If they do end up at a club, it's hard for them to find someone worth talking to. The loud music and talking at bars and clubs make it impossible for Sincere flirts to have a meaningful conversation. Their goal is to try to get to know people, and most clubs are no good for that purpose.

However, the main reason Sincere flirts don't like the singles scene is that they don't think that a bar or club is a good place to meet someone. They doubt that anyone worthwhile hangs out in bars. They especially doubt that anyone in a club is open to a long-term relationship. Sincere flirts have a difficult time meeting new people because, from their perspective, people at bars aren't looking for anything serious. Part of the problem is that Sincere flirts don't have much self-confidence when it comes to picking up the opposite sex in that environment. They don't want to approach strangers, even attractive strangers. They just don't know what to say in that sort of place.

THE SURVEY SAYS

Sincere flirts consider their friends to be pretty good at flirting, and they think they aren't very good at it, compared to their friends.

We all know that pickup lines are sort of corny. A close friend of mine once said, "If it is a line, then it is phony by definition." But they are still a pretty harmless way to start a conversation. As you might guess, the Sincere flirt won't use a pickup line to start a conversation. Those who are low on the Sincere flirting style are 14 percent more likely to use a pickup line than someone who is high on the Sincere style. And Sincere women *hate* strategies like teasing, sarcastic banter and jokes at their expense. That pretty much eliminates another type of strategy for getting a conversation started. Overall, Sincere flirts can't stand what goes on in bars. That just isn't a game they want to play.

THE SURVEY SAYS

Sincere flirts are 31 percent *less* likely to lie to somebody to get them interested.

DO NICE GUYS FINISH LAST?

The phrase *Nice guys finish last* may have already occurred to you more than a few times while reading this chapter. You may be asking yourself a couple of things: Is the Sincere flirt the same thing as the nice guy or the nice girl? And do nice people really finish last? The answers are (1) yes, and (2) maybe, but it depends on what they are looking for.

Several studies have explored the "nice guy" stereotype. Comparing the nice guy to the jerk has revealed that the nice guy has the following characteristics: he is pleasant and fun, he backs off when a woman isn't interested and he avoids being too direct or aggressive. The jerk is aggressive, direct and, although he can be fun, he is also a little dangerous and cold. Whether a woman prefers a nice guy to a jerk depends on what she wants. Women who want to get involved with a nice guy tend to prefer respectful, nonaggressive men. Women who are looking for an exclusive, committed relationship *really* want a nice guy.

Jerks, on the other hand, tend to be the man of choice for women who are looking for low-commitment one-night stands. In fact, jerks are exemplified by men who are cold and unfriendly and who tend to be persistent and determined when they pursue women—quite the opposite of the Sincere flirt. There is a very good reason to believe that the nice guy discovered in past research is pretty much the embodiment of the Sincere flirt. So do they really finish last?

RESEARCH SAYS

You can tell if a guy is a jerk by his pickup line: if it is direct, sexual and overly complimentary, then the guy is probably conceited and fickle.

If you think that finishing last includes seeking out and getting into long-term relationships, not hooking up with a lot of different sexual partners and respecting that *no* really does mean no, then Sincere flirts really do finish last. Dead last in comparison to the jerks. But if you think that a person's flirting style can help her get what she wants out of a relationship, that a person's flirting style can tell you a lot about what she desires in a partner and a relationship, and that slowly developing intimate relationships can be a good thing, then Sincere flirts finish first. Basically, nice guys finish last in the race for expedient casual sex. And that isn't a bad race to lose in my book.

SEX, RELATIONSHIPS AND LOVE

RESEARCH SAYS

Both men and women have sex to create a stronger emotional bond.

Sex

So far, I have given you some hints about what Sincere flirts really think about sex. If you guessed that they'd really prefer it to be in the context of a romantic relationship, then you got it pretty well nailed (no pun intended). According to the FSI Survey, both men and women with a Sincere style of flirting have had fewer past sexual partners and fewer one-night stands. Additionally, Sincere flirts are 19 percent less likely to have dated multiple people at the same time. So far, so good. What is really interesting is that the Sincere style has a lot more to do with men's sexual attitudes than it does women's. Why? The answer is in the script.

PLAY YOUR PART

We have a script for doing a lot of things—going to the grocery store, paying our bill at a restaurant, even going on
a date. A script is basically a sequence of events that leads down
a particular path, ending at a particular goal. In the case of
the sexual script, it usually follows a very gender-specific
path. Specifically, men are expected to take the lead on
nearly everything—approaching a woman, buying her a drink,
asking about her interests, touching her, asking if she wants
"to get out of here" and, once alone, initiating kissing and
eventually initiating sex. This is all because women are supposed to be the gatekeepers and men are supposed to be
the aggressors.

When a guy is a Sincere flirt, he doesn't follow this script.
He isn't overly aggressive and he isn't pushy about sex. Just
like Andrew, he doesn't approach and put the moves on women.
In the case of casual sex, Sincere men act in a way that runs
against their official role as the aggressor. Sincere men tend
to have a much more careful and puritanical attitude about
sex. They think sex outside of a relationship is inappropriate
and they don't think sex without love is OK. By believing those
things, Sincere men are acting against their script.

This puts men with a highly Sincere style in a bind. They
have respectful attitudes about sex and very cautious attitudes
about pursuing women. Despite some frustrations, they also
think that this is a good thing. They believe that women will
respect and be attracted to a man who is less pushy. It is important to keep in mind that having a Sincere style of flirting doesn't
mean you don't want sex. Sexual desire is simply unrelated to

a Sincere style of flirting. So don't confuse a Sincere flirting style with chastity.

ROLE REVERSAL

For the Sincere flirt, especially a man, it is going to take a woman who is willing to go against her sexual script and initiate. Think of it this way—the Sincere flirt wants to have sex, but he just wants to do so in the context of a relationship. So how do the Sincere flirt and his prospective partner start a relationship? By building intimacy quickly through talking, sharing and self-disclosing. Once they get to talking, though, it might not be clear to *anyone* that this is getting anyone anywhere nearer to having sex. The Sincere man might need a woman who is a little more assertive to move the relationship to the next level.

Relationships

Once in a relationship, people with the Sincere flirting style have important and meaningful relationships. When asked about their last romantic relationship, they said it was no casual fling; it was the real deal. They described their last partner in exceedingly positive terms: physically attractive, interesting, fun and emotionally close and connected. It seems that being an ex-boyfriend or ex-girlfriend of a Sincere flirt is a pretty good deal, too. They liked you in the relationship, and still consider you a valued friend after you break up. So why did you break up again? Just kidding...

Love

Sincere flirts experience love in a very idealized way. They generally seek out love that is called *agape* or pure, selfless love. They don't want to play games or play the field. They want a lover who is willing to make sacrifices, to endure difficulties, to be in it for the long haul.

The goal of the Sincere flirt is intimacy. A social psychology researcher named Catherine Sanderson identified people who wanted to experience the warmth, closeness and intimacy of relationships. These were people who truly enjoyed interactions that created intimate feelings. They tended to use emotional strategies to start romantic relationships. I would say that these people are the spitting image of a Sincere flirting style. Just like the Sincere style, people who cherish being close and connected to others tend to avoid big parties. They are looking for a long-term relationship, not an expedient hookup.

RESEARCH SAYS

Men and women are equally likely to be motivated by intimacy goals.

SINCERE FLIRTS IN LOVE

Now that you have an idea of what the Sincere style is all about, I want to tell you a story of two Sincere flirts. Their romance has all of the features of a good film—star-crossed lovers, a romantic location and youthful exuberance. But it also has something unique to the Sincere style, which you soon shall see.

Lesley was tired of traveling. Her trip wasn't going exactly as planned. She decided to travel through the cities of Eastern Europe—Berlin, Budapest and Prague—to avoid the touristy elements of travel that you'd see in places like Paris, London or Rome. She wanted to experience travel, but not in the same way as everyone else.

Arriving in Prague early one morning, she was exhausted. Lesley slung her huge backpack over her shoulders one more time, and made her way to the hostel from the train station. She looked a bit worn from the wear of hopping from city to city, carrying her possessions on her back like a nomad. She was dying for a shower, but once she got to the hostel, she found out that she couldn't check in and get cleaned up for several hours. They let her store her stuff in a back room, but no shower yet.

At the coffee shop near the hostel, she settled in to try to read *Gravity's Rainbow* again, which she had promised herself she would finish before her trip was through. Pynchon was no easy read, but Lesley thought it was a challenge and maybe something entertaining to pass the time. Now she just regretted how heavy it was (both literally and literarily) after schlepping it from place to place.

Jason had been in Prague for several days. It was his favorite city of all. Its beautiful old-world character and sense of a place lost in time felt, well, romantic to him. Not to say that Jason was looking for romance in Prague, just that his personality was well-suited for travel. He found it easy to pass the time with fellow travelers, to share stories and to ask questions. The experience of being thrown into a new place, not even being able to speak the language—this was exciting to Jason. He had been at the café for the morning, and when he saw Lesley walk in, he figured that she was probably an American and she was probably new here, too.

"What's that you're reading?" asked Jason. Lesley didn't look up, but raised the book up so he could see the cover. "A little light reading for the road?" he joked.

Lesley smiled to herself, regretting her choice to bring something so heavy. Then she looked up at Jason, and she liked what she saw. He had that slightly unkempt and extremely laid-back look of most of the men she had fallen for in the past. He was tall and thin, skinny even, but not in the least unattractive. Lesley immediately regretted the bandanna holding her hair back, her two days without a shower and her choice *not* to at least change the shirt she had slept in the night before.

"Well, I thought that if I were going to travel, I might as well get the most exercise I could," Lesley replied. "Unlike rocks, I thought, at least I can read this, but I haven't made much progress."

"I'm Jason," he said, sticking out his hand, "part of the Prague welcoming committee."

"I'm Lesley, delighted to be the recipient of your service."

Jason sat down, and they began to talk.

RESEARCH SAYS

The more comfortable you feel talking with people, the more they will like you. And vice versa.

They talked about books and traveling and being alone. They talked about people they'd met on the way and hoped to see again, and those they'd left behind and were glad to abandon. Jason shared his love of travel, and Lesley explained her decision to come to Eastern and not Western Europe. Soon, they both had the feeling that they had been talking for a while. Like waking up from a long, restful nap, they checked the time and found that hours had passed. Lesley said she wanted to get back to the hostel, and Jason offered to show her around Prague when she was up for it. Lesley quickly went up to her room and changed her clothes. Suddenly, she remembered that she had forgotten to shower. She took a look in the mirror at her stringy hair and bandanna, smiled and said, "Screw that" and took off to find Jason.

Happy to see her, Jason vaguely waved at Lesley as she made her way through the lobby. Once in earshot, he grinned, "Back so soon?"

They walked and talked. They ate and talked. And they drank and talked. Each conversation felt like something new and exciting. They felt as if they were learning everything at once, and wished that all the little wonderful details could come even faster. It felt amazing to be so close to someone after a long wait enforced by the solitude of backpacking.

They challenged each other and made each other think. They shared ideas that were well-worn and ones they had only told close friends before that night. Each cherished each response because Jason and Lesley felt that everything was both new and familiar at the same time.

They spent that evening and far into the early morning hours together, seeking out new places to discover both in the city and in each other's thoughts and dreams. Jason wished that he had met her long before that day, and Lesley wished the same. It was like disrobing emotionally and finding out that you liked how the other person looked naked.

Chapter Six

THE TRADITIONAL STYLE

Imagine that you are interviewing a couple of Traditional flirts. Think of yourself as the interviewer asking questions about their perspective on flirting and dating.

Q: Walk me through your typical evening out.

Katie: When I go out, it is important to me to look my best. These days, girls don't wear heels and dresses as much as they used to, but they are my favorite. Heels make me feel more feminine, more girlish and sexier. When it comes to dresses, nothing revealing, of course. You know, first impressions really matter!

William: You know the saying, Clothes make the man? Well, I totally believe that, so I sometimes can go a bit overboard getting ready. I've got to make sure my hair is just right. Then, its Boss shirts and pants, and always cologne. I try to dress better than any other guy I'm going out with.

Q: When you go out, where you do and your friends usually go?

Katie: The perfect place for me is someplace classy, like the places you see in the movies. My friends like to go to clubs to meet guys, but I just can't stand the idea of putting myself out there like that. We usually compromise on a place that is more low-key, like a hotel bar or someplace more relaxed.

William: I'm up for whatever, but some places I like more than others. My friends and I like to go to this cigar lounge before we head out somewhere. I sometimes wish that you could meet women there, but it is all dudes. It is my kind of place, you know? A place you can get a cigar and a scotch. Afterwards, we hit clubs where the drinks are expensive and there is a line out front. That's my kind of place.

Q: Tell me about how you go about approaching someone you are interested in.

Katie: There is a rule I never break: I don't approach guys. Some girls are aggressive and I have no problem with that, but it's just not for me. The guy should show he is interested. I don't want to put myself out there and get shot down. I'd much rather have a guy make the first move.

William: I heard once that the best pickup line is a simple hello, and I totally agree. I walk up, put my hand out and introduce myself. Just like that. I don't just walk up to a girl and ask her if she wants a drink. Some guys do it and it works for them, but I'm not one of those guys. I want to get to know her. That way she knows I'm not trying to get her drunk. She has to show me that she is someone I want to buy a drink for.

Q: Do you have any rules about how people should act when they are flirting?

Katie: For guys? A big one for me is eye contact, smiling, being interesting and acting interested. I hate it when guys get distracted by other girls. Another rule for me is no touching. If it is a guy I've just met, I don't want him to touch me. He should be a gentleman. I guess maybe a light touch on my arm is OK, but a guy shouldn't be all grabby. Actually, that rule applies to women, too.

William: I tell my friends all the time, when you are talking with girls, you want to talk about *her*. Make sure she's comfortable while you're there. When I talk to a woman, my goal is to comfort her. I want to show her I could take care of her, if necessary.

Q: What do you expect on a first date?

Katie: I think that a lot of guys these days don't believe in opening doors and giving compliments, but I still think that a guy picking up the check is really sweet. It isn't just about showing that he is interested, it shows that he knows how to treat a lady. It helps me tell a good guy from a bad one. How he behaves around women is one of the first indicators for me. One time I had a guy take me to a really nice place and he ordered for both of us. I thought that was pretty classy.

William: I am 100 percent a gentleman when it comes to dating. Whatever people say, men should still take the lead. You gotta be polite, you gotta hold the door, you gotta pull the chair out. I absolutely believe that guys should pick up the tab—at least on the first few dates. Actually, you know what? On all of them. Every single girl I go on a date with tries to pay, but that's not how I was brought up. You know another big one? Standing up when a girl leaves the table. I think that one really shows respect.

Q: What do you think makes people good at flirting?

Katie: It's funny that you would ask that because I know I wouldn't say the same thing as a lot of other girls. A lot of girls my age think it is OK to approach guys. I would never ask a guy out on a date or chase him. In my opinion, it just makes you look cheap. A lady is a better flirt when she is more reserved and keeps him guessing. So I tend to play the shy card for a lot longer than most girls I know. Part of being a good flirt is letting a guy show you what he is all about. I will wait a few seconds to give a guy a chance to pull out my chair or open a door for me. I don't know any woman who wouldn't want that.

William: When it comes to conversation, I am definitely a listener. I would love to tell her about myself, but I don't want to sound cocky. I listen 90 percent of the time and talk 10 percent of the time. It isn't just about listening, though. When my 10 percent time comes, I make sure she knows I am confident and in control. Girls like it when a guy takes control of a situation and lets them know what is going to happen next. You have got to be charming, but you have got to be fearless, too.

Even though they play different roles in courtship, Katie and William share similar views on the ways of romance. The two of them are Traditional flirts and they both have a crystal-clear understanding about how men and women ought to act. These two things—courtship and men's and women's separate roles in it—are central elements of the Traditional flirting style. As you will see, the Traditional flirting style is all about how men and women *ought to* interact.

WHAT IS THE TRADITIONAL FLIRTING STYLE?

~~~~~~

The Traditional style taps into the strongly held belief that there is one way of communicating attraction, a way that has always been and will always be. Like Polite flirts, Traditional flirts believe that there are rules that guide how men and women behave during courtship. More importantly, they believe there are rules about how men and women *ought to* act in general: women should be ladies and men should be gentlemen. The Traditional flirting style measures whether you believe in this Traditional arrangement or not.

Whether a man or woman, a Traditional flirt thinks that it is up to the man to take control when initiating a relationship. Simply put, men should make the first move and women should not pursue men. By way of comparison, those who are low in the Traditional style are more likely to believe that it really doesn't matter who initiates a relationship and it's OK for a woman to be assertive.

RESEARCH SAYS

Men who have a stereotypically masculine personality will take control of courtship by being direct and forward.

Traditional flirts believe in separate roles for men and women when it comes to courtship and, for that matter, a good many other things. This set of beliefs about courtship not only guides their own behavior, but it influences how they see other people. Like Katie and William, Traditional flirts have strong rules for themselves, and these rules apply to other people as well. William gets angry at less Traditional guys who are not gentlemanly, and Katie looks down on women she thinks are being too forward. The Traditional style is tied up in tightly defined rules for men and women: men are at their best when they behave in a bold and manly fashion and women are at their best when they are feminine and demure.

How to Spot a Traditional Flirt

1. Traditional flirts believe in the tried-and-true methods of romance.
2. Traditional flirts rarely become romantically involved with their friends.
3. Traditional men can be found on internet dating sites.
4. If you met at the club, both of you might be Traditional flirts.
5. If you feel like you are in a fairy-tale romance, or want to be in one, then you are probably a Traditional flirt.
6. You might be a Traditional flirt if you think that in an ideal relationship the man is the breadwinner and the woman is a housewife.
7. If a woman is being intentionally or strategically vague about her attraction or interest in a guy, then she is probably a Traditional flirt.
8. During a date, a Traditional man will follow his role to a T: opening doors, pulling away the chair and insisting or even arguing that he pays the check.

9. During a date, a Traditional woman will hold back, be a bit reserved and somewhat nervous, not putting herself out there. These are all signs that she wants a man to come on strong.

10. Traditional flirts find a little jealousy to be an exciting part of keeping chemistry alive.

WHO IS A TRADITIONAL FLIRT?

Women, Absolutely Women

As you might have guessed, men are *much* more likely than women to hope that women will make the first move. As a consequence, the Traditional style is *much* more common among women than men. In terms of the overall prevalence of the five styles, women are Sincere and Polite flirts first, then, after that, the Traditional flirting style is tied for third with Playful and Physical. This means that if you picked a woman out of a crowd, she is just as likely to be a Traditional flirt as a Playful or Physical flirt. For men, the Traditional style is dead last—a distant fifth behind the other four styles of flirting. When it comes right down to it, most men are pretty open to being approached by women. Men think that women who initiate a conversation—and especially physical contact—are more seductive and more open to having sex. This means that a Traditional flirting style in a man is pretty rare.

However, whether men (or women) like it or not, the Traditional style of flirting is built into the DNA of classic American dating life. People know that, traditionally, it is a man's duty to be assertive and a woman's role to be coy and at least a little resistant to a man's pursuit. People believe this to be true even if they don't actually behave this way themselves! The Traditional flirting style is so much a part of how we go about initiating a date that if you don't act in a Traditional way you might miss out, no matter whether you are a man or a woman.

Men who aren't at least a little Traditional are probably missing out on a lot of potential dates, especially when they are college-aged. Most women are simply unlikely to approach men who don't take at least some sort of proactive role. On the other hand, women who are not at least a little Traditional may face some unfortunate, but very real, consequences. A woman who is a little too aggressive can potentially damage her reputation. If a non-Traditional woman approached a Traditional man, it would probably turn out poorly. He'd see her as promiscuous or loose and she'd be irritated and offended by the judgment: "That guy is *waaaay* too old-fashioned for my taste."

18–24-Year-Olds

Now this one is a shocker. The Traditional style is about Traditional gender roles. Even the name of the style—*Traditional*—implies that it is the way prior generations flirted. However, to give you a picture of just how much more Traditional young adults are than other age groups, the age group that ranked closest behind 18-24-year-olds in the Traditional Style was 25-29-year-olds, and they were significantly less Traditional than the 18-24-year-olds. Even men, who were across the board less Traditional flirts than women, were higher in the Traditional style at 18-24 than at *any other time in their life*. Older men weren't even close. Why are young people embracing these old ways of courtship?

As I mentioned earlier, the Traditional style is all about following a script about what men and women *ought* to do when flirting. Traditional flirts believe that men should ask women out, and buy a woman a drink or pick up the tab at dinner. They believe that women should never be the aggressor. Men come on to women and, if he is gentlemanly enough, women consent to being pursued. Men approach and women passively go along with it. It is not that she doesn't want his attention or that she doesn't play a role in keeping him coming back for more. She just can't be too aggressive or forward in doing so. The bottom line is that Traditional flirts not only believe in this script, they practice what they preach.

There are two main reasons that young adults would be so Traditional. The first is a matter of choice and the second is a matter of effectiveness. There is simply *nothing* like college and young adulthood when it comes to choice. Not only are there thousands and thousands of other young adults on a typical college campus, they are constantly replenishing their ranks. Seniors graduate and next fall a new batch of freshmen arrive. The young-adult singles scene is similar: there are always new people to meet, get to know and ask out.

While it may be obvious, it bears repeating: young people are much more likely to be single than older people! As a consequence of all these choices, women can wait a while for men to approach. They can be choosy with men they meet because new eligible bachelors are behind doors number 2, 3, 4, 5, 6…and on and on.

The second reason that the Traditional style is so high among young adults is that the Traditional dating script is much more effective for young people than for older adults. By setting down some pretty clear guidelines about how to approach someone and who does what to whom, two potential lovers can take the road more traveled. By comparison, mature women don't wait around for some guy to approach. They tend to take a more active role in courtship.

Now men are generally more open to women being the aggressor throughout life. But, for men as well as women, the Traditional style gets lower and lower as they age. This probably happens as a matter of choice, too. When there are fewer available women to meet and date, men—even ones with more Traditional attitudes about courtship—are open to women approaching them. If women approach, it makes it thankfully obvious.

I had a friend who had a very Traditional flirting style. He had never been married before and didn't meet his wife until he was in his early 40s. After they had known each other and worked together for several *years*, she finally told him point blank that he should ask her out. She may have been the aggressor in that case, but she told him she was available so she could start formally dating. And he was just fine with that.

RESEARCH SAYS

In the early 1900s, women invited men to call on them at the woman's home. Men asking whether they could call was considered unseemly.

Old-Fashioned and Predictable Personality

It should be obvious by now that a Traditional flirt is pretty old-fashioned when it comes to romance. What is interesting is that when you look at the personality of Traditional flirts, they are also pretty predictable people in general. They are not terribly open to changes or new opportunities. They will pick their favorite restaurant over a new one every time. They'd prefer to do something they know and can count on, rather than something new and trendy. The Traditional flirt likes to stick to the tried-and-true things in life, not just in the land of love.

Complementary Styles

The Polite (see page 57) and Traditional styles are often confused for one another. This is because people think that Traditional flirting is Polite, and Polite flirting is Traditional. Both men and women who advocate a more Traditional approach to courtship do tend to believe that courtship is rule-governed. What really distinguishes the two is that although a Polite flirt acts the same whether a man or a woman, a Traditional man and a Traditional woman act in very different ways. For example, women who are Traditional flirts are very unlikely to be Playful flirts (see page 81), but this is not the case if they are men. This makes sense. Traditional men could be Playful or not. In being the aggressor in courtship, men could take on a devil-may-care attitude. They can be charming, fun and even play little games. But, a Traditional woman believes in Traditional gender roles, which means that too in-your-face and fun-loving ways of flirting by women are considered overly forward or unladylike.

THE SURVEY SAYS

The Traditional guy doesn't really see himself as a big flirt, and he believes that his friends are much better at it than he is.

DATING, SEX AND LOVE

The Traditional flirting style is about how men and women *ought* to behave when communicating attraction. What does the Traditional style say about your dating and sex life and your attitudes about love? Well, it depends on whether you are a man or a woman.

Women who think that men should approach them are upholding Traditional, but relatively common, attitudes about courtship for women. Men who insist that men should pursue women (and not the other way around) are few in number and have very constrained ideas about how dating ought to go. They are also more unique among men. As a consequence, there are a lot of differences between Traditional male and female flirts. To proceed, first we'll talk about the way the Traditional flirt views the relationship between men and women. Then, the sorts of things that are specific to *only* Traditional men or *only* Traditional women will be covered. After that, I'll give you a rundown of all of the similarities between men and women for the Traditional style of flirting.

Chivalry and Control

I recently met a young woman from the Middle East who was studying in the United States. She was fascinated to learn about how flirting works in the United States because it was so different in her own country. In the Middle East, there are strict rules about what kinds of clothing women can wear and what sorts of things they can do. There are also pretty strict rules about how courtship is initiated. Hearing her story gave me some insight into what things were like long ago in the United States.

IT'S A MAN'S WORLD

In the Middle East, it is pretty common for the bride's and groom's families to play a central role in deciding to whom a woman will be wed. Male members of both families—fathers, grandfathers, uncles and brothers—will meet together to discuss the union of the two families. The groom comes with his entourage of male kin, but the prospective bride and her mother are not invited. This is all done because Middle Eastern cultures place a high premium on protecting women, especially protecting their virtue and chastity.

BUT IT WOULD MEAN NOTHING WITHOUT A WOMAN

In the United States, there once was a similar phenomenon. American families were once heavily involved in choosing who their sons and daughters married. Until the arrival of the automobile and the emergence of youth culture in the 1940s and 1950s, a young male suitor would be invited to "call" at the home of a local girl. The young lady would meet with the young man under the watchful eyes of her parents, especially her father. All these rules were put in place to try to protect women and shelter them from potential ruin at the hands of (read: evil) men. When *dating* (the term was new slang in 1914) replaced calling, it took women out of their homes, out in public and into men's cars. Men ended up paying for dates because they had a job and money, and women often couldn't work outside the home. What is similar between early-20th-century American culture and present-day Middle Eastern culture is that in sheltering and protecting women, each culture also controls and restricts women's actions.

There are many people who like Traditional flirting and wish for a return to those times. They see the new ways of interaction between young adults as both risky and unseemly. Without question, there are real risks and consequences of less Traditional dating arrangements, such as the college hookup culture. The bigger issue at hand, however, is that the protection and idealization of women's chastity and virtue go hand in hand with limiting women's choices.

> ### Cyber-flirting
>
> Using Instant Messenger to flirt leaves Traditional flirts cold and unsatisfied.

DELICATE FLOWERS AND MANLY PROVIDERS

Throughout the world, this same pattern emerges. In more traditional societies, where there is a strict separation between the sexes, women's lives are more tightly constrained. In more egalitarian societies, women and men mingle freely and women make their own way in the world. When a society is more traditional, people see women as beautiful, delicate flowers who need protection. People in more traditional societies see women as more virtuous than men and in dire need of rescuing from the perils of society and, of course, dangerous men. In more traditional cultures, heroic men want to play the role of gallant knight who rescues a damsel in distress.

The Traditional flirt embraces all these things. Whether they are men or women, Traditional flirts are off the charts in believing that men are at their best when they are knights in shining armor. They idealize and revere women as princesses, ladies and damsels. It is very easy to see how these beliefs about men's and women's roles in society have clear overtones about how courtship ought to be conducted. What this means for courtship is that the roles of men and women are clear-cut, well-established and ought to be respected.

Beauty and Riches

Let me give you a few examples of how this all works out in practice. I'm sure you have heard that men want a beautiful wife and women want a rich husband. There is good evidence that, when asked to say what they want in a future wife or husband, men *do* value beauty in a partner more than women do and women *do* value wealth and success in a partner more than men do. For the Traditional flirt, however, this is particularly true. In fact, they take it up a notch. The Traditional man is quite agreeable to having a trophy wife. It may even be his express goal when he tries to meet women. Similarly, the Traditional woman may be seeking her Mrs. degree in college (you know, to become *Mrs.* Smith or *Mrs.* Johnson). Her education is secondary to the quality of men she meets. Traditional flirts believe that this arrangement is how it ought to be. Traditional flirts do not mind it if a man wants to have a trophy wife. Not only do they not mind, Traditional women might be thrilled if they were the ones chosen to fulfill that role.

RESEARCH SAYS

In the late 1950s, two-thirds of women who started college dropped out, usually to get married.

Clear Trade-offs

What the Traditional flirt doesn't like is people who stray from those roles a bit too far. The Traditional flirt isn't too keen on having or being a househusband. The Traditional flirt does not like a woman who is open and agreeable to having casual sex. In fact, if a woman is both a Polite and a Traditional flirt, she would strongly condemn such an "easy" woman.

For women, particularly, agreeing to these restrictions gets them something good in return—protection, provision, esteem and idealization. For men, this trade-off gets them something, too—control, power and a feeling of being valued. Whatever your own values or attitudes about how women and men ought to be in society, there is no question that each perspective offers costs and benefits.

If Traditional flirts were confronted with the criticism that these ways of thinking might keep men in places of control and women in places of submission in society, they'd either be agreeable with that trade-off or they'd become irritated that something or someone made all these traditional arrangements so messy and unclear. The roles of women and men are time-tested, the Traditional flirt would say, and ought to be respected.

Separation (Not Battle) of the Sexes

One way to think about all this is to think about what it means to be a man with a Traditional flirting style or a woman with a Traditional flirting style. In some ways they are very different and in some ways very similar.

THE SURVEY SAYS

Because Traditional women may be a little anxious about starting new relationships, they may appear more distant and nervous when first meeting a guy.

TRADITIONAL WOMEN

How do these beliefs play out in Traditional women's dating lives? Well, flirting for Traditional women is a bit of a challenge. Because they avoid being too aggressive, the very act of flirting is, well, rare. Female Traditional flirts don't flirt with men in whom they are interested, and they don't like it very much when men flirt with them, either. When a Traditional woman recognizes that a man is flirting with her, she doesn't find it very flattering and won't flirt back.

The Traditional woman is choosy and believes that very few men have real dating potential. She is so passive, in fact, that when she does actually attempt to flirt with someone she likes, she doesn't feel very successful or confident in doing so. Like a lady of the 1950s, a Traditional woman doesn't seek out a private and personal conversation with a guy. As a consequence, when a Traditional woman is actually interested in a guy, she has trouble getting him to notice her. She won't approach strangers, even attractive ones. Even during that conversation, she doesn't tend to seek out information about whether or not he is open or available to a relationship. After all, that is a man's job. Apparently, the limited role represented in her Traditional beliefs leaves few options for attracting a guy, which leads to less success when she tries to do so. As a consequence, Traditional women find it frustrating to meet new people.

THE SURVEY SAYS

The Traditional style is the only flirting style where women are intentionally vague when flirting.

Where Traditional Women Find Love

When Traditional women go out, they want to feel attractive and get noticed. Well, that is sort of tricky when they don't like to flirt themselves and don't think it is very flattering to be hit on. Traditional women don't like going to bars, because they don't believe that bars offer a path to a committed relationship. But they do like going to clubs. That's because the club scene is a little more about looking good than it is about meeting people. When Traditional women seek the attentions of men through their looks, they do it for the sake of self-esteem that comes with a guy being interested. She isn't really interested in learning about him or about whether a relationship might grow from that conversation. A Traditional lady has a few things in her arsenal to get a guy's attention or to try to get that hit of self-esteem. The FSI Survey indicated that Traditional women were willing to use their feminine wiles to attract a guy. Specifically, they were 11 percent more likely than their non-Traditional counterparts to lie to attract a potential boyfriend. A little deception might work in her favor when trying to make a guy fall for her.

RESEARCH SAYS

Women, but not men, think that being passive when flirting is both effective and flirtatious.

TRADITIONAL MEN

Traditional men have very different experiences in flirting. A man with a Traditional flirting style is looking for a lady who is demure and passive, yielding and subtle. She must be responsive to his attentions, but only slightly so—never too direct or clearly interested. Like Traditional women, he feels attracted to only a few potential partners. A Traditional man is quite selective in whom he approaches and will wait until an existing relationship is established before flirting with a woman. Consequently, Traditional men often know a lady for a long time before approaching her. He will put his lady on a pedestal, which may make a girl feel good and leave her wanting a little more. But this may also leave her in the dark about whether he is actually interested or not.

Where Traditional Men Find Love

It appears that Traditional men also go to clubs to meet women. True to their gender script, Traditional guys are more likely to approach attractive women. I imagine that this is a bit of a challenge for Traditional women who'd like to meet Traditional guys. Because a Traditional lady isn't putting herself out there sexually and men typically won't approach women they don't at least share eye contact with, this means a Traditional guy may be unlikely to approach a Traditional woman. More than any other flirting style, the Traditional guy feels that he has to work to get women interested in him. Perhaps part of the reason is that he'd like to take it slow, given his traditional nature.

THE SURVEY SAYS

A Traditional man uses traditional means to achieve his goal. Traditional men are 18 percent more likely to use a pickup line than a non-Traditional man.

The internet can be a very good place for Traditional men to find love. According to the FSI Survey, Traditional men were 22 percent more likely to have used the internet to meet their last girlfriend. The internet may allow Traditional men to find an avenue to slowly build a relationship before acting. Interestingly, this preference for the internet doesn't apply to Traditional women. Perhaps their lack of openness to new experiences prevents them from seeking out a partner there. Or maybe Traditional women believe the myths that all the men on internet dating sites are married, trolling for an affair. In either case, Traditional women would find it advantageous to check out internet dating as a way to meet Traditional men.

CYBER-FLIRTING

When Traditional men communicate with women online, they often will overestimate women's interest.

DATING AND RELATIONSHIPS

What unites Traditional men and Traditional women? What do they have in common? The better way to think about this is to consider how a Traditional man and a Traditional woman might interact. It seems there are two possibilities: the slow go and the gallant stranger.

The Slow Go

A Traditional man would not find many women in whom he was interested. If the Traditional man found a woman to whom he felt strongly attracted, he would be hesitant to approach her. He would want to establish a respectful and cordial relationship before approaching this lucky lady. Perhaps, then, he would develop a strong but nonromantic acquaintanceship. And only then, after things were more settled, would he act on his romantic desires. During that time, a Traditional woman would be unreceptive to his flirtation, unlikely to approach her suitor, and would not directly communicate her attraction to him. Once they have finally communicated their interest in each other, then and only then would they seek a more personal and private conversation.

THE SURVEY SAYS

Traditional men and women often rely on a friend to help get things started. Both say that they have had an experience where they didn't know someone was interested in them until a friend intervened.

The Gallant Stranger

Because a Traditional man also might be a guy who sees himself as a prince in a fairy tale, he might play the part of a gallant stranger. As I said before, the Traditional style tells us less about what a guy is going to do than what a woman is going to do. In the case of pathways to romance, the Traditional man is equally likely to be slow or to be passionately direct. We have considered the slow-go approach, now what about a more assertive path?

In my research with Melanie Canterberry, we looked at whether or not men used strategies that were competitive and persistent, assertive and isolating, and teasing and joking. In the case of Traditional men and women, they both felt the teasing strategies were distasteful. They thought these frivolous strategies were demeaning to a woman, rather than holding her in high esteem. Revealingly, both Traditional men and Traditional women simply loved the idea of a guy competing with other men for a woman's affections. Like Sir Lancelot, torn by his love for Guinevere and his king, the Traditional man may find himself drawn to a woman so passionately that he is willing to compete with any other suitor. If a Traditional woman sees this, she loves it! It shows that he has the mettle and fortitude to meet her desires. Rather than returning his affections directly or passionately, she will respond demurely, tacitly allowing the competition (or "sword" fight) to commence. It is a boost to her self-worth and -esteem that two men want her so desperately that they will fight for her. Each one wants to take her from that place and take her home with him and him alone. Whew!

SEX, RELATIONSHIPS AND LOVE

Sex, Traditionally

Having a Traditional flirting style directly translates into having a conservative attitude about sex. The Traditional flirt believes that sex should take place only within the context of a committed, long-term relationship, preferably a marriage. This belief applies to Traditional flirts, whether they are men or women. Consistent with those beliefs, Traditional men and women also have had fewer sexual partners in the past. But Traditional women have even stronger beliefs about the sacredness of sex than do men. This is consistent with the classic double standard where Traditional men could "sow their wild oats," but if Traditional women did so, they would be sullied, corrupted or demeaned.

According to the FSI Survey, if a Traditional woman ends up having sex with a man, she may do so for the purpose of trying to establish a more committed relationship. One way to look at this is that because she believes that sex is so strongly tied to a long-term relationship, she perceives that because she had sex, it must mean that the relationship is budding. Another way to see it is that she wants to protect her virtue. If she does end up succumbing to her desires, she may want to start a serious romantic relationship with a man to keep up appearances.

The Survey Says

Traditional women are 20 percent more likely to say that they have used sex as a way to try to get a man interested in a long-term relationship.

Relationships

When Traditional flirts are asked to describe their most recent relationship, they show themselves to be very committed partners. They do not get into any relationship lightly—no casual flings for either Traditional men or Traditional women. Interestingly, they do not experience love at first sight very often, either. When they met their last relationship partner, they didn't know they were going to have a relationship with that person. However, once they start a romantic relationship, they tend to stay put. The good news is that their flirting style stops them from hunting around for new partners while in a relationship. Traditional flirts were 20 percent less likely to flirt with someone else while in a long-term relationship. However, you can't quite describe their last relationship as being full of fireworks, bells and whistles. Theirs is a much more staid and calm way of loving.

Love

Men and women who are Traditional flirts are very similar to one another when it comes to matters of love. The way Traditional flirts love is very similar to their way of flirting. Again, just as in the case of attracting a partner, there seem to be two pathways to love—the slow go and the gallant stranger.

THE SLOW GO

The Traditional flirt is the most likely of any of the flirting styles to have a pragmatic approach when it comes to love. Remember how Middle Eastern families see romance as a union of two households? Well, this same idea applies to love for the Traditional flirting style. Traditional flirts look for things about a prospective partner that might ensure their happiness and comfort in a relationship: that she comes from a good family or she has a good upbringing, that he is wealthy or attractive, or that she will make a good parent. It makes sense that people who flirt slowly, carefully and with a very Traditional style of communicating attraction will also make prudent and careful choices about whom they fall in love with.

What also fits with this slow-go path is the fact that Traditional flirts had less emotional and physical chemistry in their last romantic relationship. For women, being very Traditional may actually decrease physical chemistry. Perhaps they are concerned with the rational and realistic aspects of love, not the more frivolous aspects, which then diminish their emotional experience. Perhaps they are very concerned with maintaining a chaste and wholesome demeanor, even in a committed relationship, which decreases their sexual chemistry.

THE GALLANT STRANGER

The theme of princes rescuing damsels in distress comes up again and again in the Traditional style of flirting. The Traditional style of flirting is more likely than any other style to experience the highest highs and the lowest lows in courtship. They experience what is called *manic* love. For them, love is a way of being rescued from unpleasant or maybe even downright awful circumstances. They hold an escapist view of love. Think Julia Roberts in *Pretty Woman*. She really wanted the whole love story, not just part of it. Manic lovers believe that love will solve your problems. All you need is the right person to come along and every problem will recede into the background. Love will conquer all. (Keep in mind that love is conquering, destroying or overcoming all things—not saving, investing or protecting the lovers.)

On this gallant stranger path, when romance begins it is incredibly exciting and enticing. But as it progresses, it brings pain. The jealousy of sharing your lover's time with his or her friends will bother the Traditional flirt. Worse yet, women who are Traditional flirts also bring a bit of a game-player mentality to relationships. Remember how I said that Traditional women might act a little coy or use deception to try to get a man interested? Well, once in a relationship with their gallant prince, they want to keep him close. To do so, a Traditional woman knows that his passions are aroused by competition with other men, and she may use little tricks to inspire those passions. She might resort to telling little lies or doing things that will inspire his jealousy and, preferably, his protection.

For the Traditional man, rather than being upset by these tactics, he endures them boldly and bravely. Not only does he see love as an act of self-sacrifice, he wants to rescue his damsel from her distress. He will patiently wait out the games and ploys because he knows that she needs his protection and may need a strong shoulder to cry on when it is all settled. He will, in short, be called upon to be a man for the sake of his lover.

TRADITIONAL FLIRTS IN LOVE

Because of their mutually shared beliefs about courtship, Traditional flirts are made for each other. I have a story that reveals the gallant prince avenue of attraction.

Victoria was bored. When she first met Henry she thought she was dreaming. Henry was a young stockbroker with a BMW; exceptional taste in wine, food, and clothes; and Henry wanted Victoria—desperately. At least it seemed that way early on. They were swept up in a fantasy romance, with flowers and gifts and trips. But now they were a couple, and that was much less exciting. Henry made great money and he let her know she could quit her job whenever she liked and move into his condo. Victoria wasn't so sure. Henry was successful, but he worked constantly and he didn't pay much attention to her. She wanted a man who treated her like a princess, put her on a pedestal and showed that he loved her desperately. These days it seemed that Henry wasn't really up to the task.

Before she met Henry, Victoria would go out with her friends to have a few drinks at her favorite hotel bar after work. She kept her job in marketing despite Henry's insistence that she quit. Although she never talked to men at bars, she was mainly there to be seen. Well, maybe she was also there to check out the local male talent. Victoria kept coming back because she liked what she saw there—lots of eligible bachelors.

Victoria never approached guys. In her view, that was poor form. She had no intention of looking as foolish as those girls who talked to guys or shamelessly flirted with them. Because her eyes were not scanning the room looking for men, Victoria never saw Walter coming. Some handsome bankers had struck up a conversation with Victoria's girlfriends. Victoria was rather cool to the whole group, and politely sipped her Cosmo as her more forward (and desperate, she thought) girlfriends talked to these men.

Just then, Walter walked up. He saw Victoria and started talking to her without introduction. He was aggressive and persistent, even after Victoria turned him down and told him she was already seeing someone. She found that captivating, even if a little irritating. Walter asked question after question about this—in his view mythical—boyfriend. Walter doubted Henry's existence and said so repeatedly. Victoria was enjoying the repartee, but she didn't tell Walter much of anything about herself. Walter backed off for the time being. Just then, Victoria's friend, Erica, came over to ask her about the hot guy she was talking to. Victoria told Erica it was nothing. Erica asked if Victoria would mind if she talked with him a bit. Victoria said, somewhat reluctantly, "Be my guest."

This was where things got interesting. Victoria relished the idea that Walter was going to have to figure out who he really wanted—Erica or her. Victoria liked that Walter had the same passion that Henry had once had. She wanted a change. She watched and she waited. She secretly wished Erica would fall on her face, and was pleased when Walter walked up to Victoria before he walked out and demanded her phone number. Victoria laughed, denied him again and Walter left alone.

Somehow, soon afterward Walter began calling her anyway. He must have coaxed Victoria's phone number from one of her friends. Slowly, but surely, Walter's persistence paid off. Victoria started answering his calls. Then, she began to distance herself from Henry. Finally, she called it off when Henry insisted that they either move in together or break up. She took door number two and never looked back.

Walter's love was a lifeline out of her boring relationship with Henry. Walter had the passion and persistence that Henry used to have, but had let die. Walter was as successful as Henry, but made time for her, too. Victoria's girlfriends envied that she had so many choices of men. From Victoria's perspective, a lady makes her own opportunities. Flirting wasn't best done by being aggressive or overtly sexy, but by demanding that a man show his worth and his mettle. And that is how she let herself be swept up by Walter. And she loved every moment of it.

 ## ASK THE DOCTOR: 28 and Done with It

Dear Dr. Hall,

I'm 28 and getting tired of the singles scene. I was a pro—I loved meeting guys. But now I feel like I'm getting too old for this. Is old-fashioned romance dead? Where do I start over to find someone more serious?

—Olivia (High on Playful and Traditional Style, Low on Polite)

Olivia, I've got some good news and some great news for you. The good news first: you are in good company. Men and women are getting married at a later age than ever before (on average nearly 27 years old for women). Yet, nearly everyone still wants to get married, have a great marriage and stay married for a long time. While you have had a change of heart about the singles scene, a ton of eligible guys are right there with you—thinking of homes and kids, rather than clubs and the next drink special.

According to your flirting style, you are a Playful flirt paired with a Traditional flirting style, and low on the Polite style. It is pretty common that women who are high in Traditional and Playful find themselves torn between their love of the game and their love of traditional romance. In some ways, this type of lady is a bit of a contradiction: she thinks it is fun to meet guys, especially ones who take control and make the first move, but she isn't that interested in settling down quite yet. Just like you, this type of woman finds that the benefits of the Playful style tend to get a little less fun as her attentions turn toward a committed relationship.

What should you do? The great news is that you have all the pieces in place to cool your Playful jets and fall back into some old-fashioned romance. Chances are, you have no problem meeting guys. You have been paying a whole lot more attention to the Playful side of your style rather than your Traditional side. Traditional guys are accustomed to approaching women, which is great for you because you know how to attract them. This is also where it probably goes awry: you are moving too fast for the Traditional guys so they will head for the hills if you start being overly Playful or forward.

Here is my advice. First, take your time. If you want romance, you've got to be patient. If a guy has already taken those first steps to talk to you, then he's interested. You want to make sure you slow it down enough for a Traditional guy to take it slow. Soak it up and let him! For a Traditional guy, taking his time is a sign that he is interested. Second, change your scene. You're over it anyway, and it's not working for you. One thing to consider is internet dating. It is a good way for Traditional types to meet one another, and Traditional men often use internet dating to find someone new. The pace might be a bit slower than you are used to, but you will find people who are a bit more serious when you shy away from your more Playful style of flirting.

Chapter Seven

THE SWITCH

It's like a switch that just turns on. I guess for me it's always on. I just have a really flirtatious personality. I'm like that every-where. Even though it might not mean I want something more, that's just how it comes off or how I come off. I don't actually try to flirt with everyone I see. It just sort of happens.

—Tyler, 23 years old

With most people, it just isn't happening. People have a right to their own space. There are so many people out there I don't care to have any romantic interest in. If that's true, there's no point in me flirting with you. Or you flirting with me, I guess. Flirting is purely for romance. I've seen people who flirt with everybody, it doesn't matter who. They just like doing it. I don't really think about flirting. Ever.

—Maria, 25 years old

Just for a moment, imagine what it would feel like to be Tyler. If you already have a flirtatious personality, as he calls it, maybe you have no trouble relating to what he is saying. Imagine what it would feel like if people were constantly tuning in to your flirtatious vibe, even when you weren't really trying. What would all of that attention feel like? Would it feel exciting? Would it be overwhelming? Would it feel fake or genuine? How would you feel about approaching someone you found attractive? Would it be easier or harder?

What if you walked a mile in Maria's shoes? Consider what it might be like to find only a few people interesting and attractive. And when you were attracted to someone, imagine what it would feel like to keep your interest safely bottled up. What if only the people you really liked could see a flirtatious side of you? Would that feel right? Would it feel secure? Would it feel dull or unexciting? How would you feel about approaching someone you liked? Confident or concerned? This is the switch, an internal button of sorts. When it's turned on, it charges up our flirting engines and makes us more receptive to others' advances. When it's off, it makes us less likely to flirt and to perceive attraction from others.

The switch isn't a matter of being good or bad at flirting. In fact, the switch has a lot to do with your flirting style. This chapter will introduce you to a new way of thinking about flirting and explain how employing the switch will make you more effective at using your own particular flirting style to your advantage.

To start, I am going to offer you three ideas that will help clarify exactly what the switch is and why it is crucial to making your flirting style work for you.

THE SWITCH IS YOUR RELATIONSHIP FRAME

Far and away the most common question people ask me is this: How do I know whether someone is flirting with me? This, my friends, is the million-dollar question. It is incredibly difficult to answer. If there is anything you have picked up from this book so far, it is the fact that everyone flirts differently. Unless someone just comes right out and says he is flirting with you (and the chances of that happening are exceedingly low), you may never know whether or not he is really flirting with you. (The long answer to this question can be found in Chapter 8, "Perceptions and Misperceptions.") Instead, because your flirting style captures how you act when you flirt, it tells the other person what type of relationship you are seeking when you flirt. The switch is all about creating a frame so you can interpret a flirtatious conversation or action.

Body Language and Ambiguity

This concept of a relationship frame is not my idea. Communication researchers have long known that body language plays a key role in making sense of the implicit relationship behind the conversation. The nonverbal part of communication, which includes everything from tone of voice to posture and eye contact, is estimated to deliver over 65 percent of the meaning in any given conversation. As the old saying goes, what you say is less important than how you say it.

Nowhere is this more important than in situations that are full of ambiguity. The thing that makes flirting so difficult to decode is that it thrives on mystery. People want to be ambiguous and indirect, play hard to get, all the while hoping that the other person correctly interprets these subtle cues. In fact, nobody ever just comes out and says, "I am attracted to you." This is because no one wants to look needy or creepy. So people use a whole arsenal of nonverbal behaviors to try to entice interest and keep it vague at the same time. Flirting is hint, hint, hinting, but saying nothing clearly.

The switch is the part of your flirting style that frames where the relationship is going. When you want to know whether a particular person is flirting, what you really want to know is, What type of relationship is this person looking for? And your switch does exactly that—it clarifies and amplifies your relationship message and your interpretation of others' messages when they're flirting.

Where do flirting styles fit in?

We know that some flirting styles are more likely to convey a message of attraction than others. The Physical style clearly frames the relationship around sexual attraction. Similarly, if you are a Playful flirt, you can use flirting to make someone do something nice for you. It frames the relationship around communicating attraction for a particular purpose (although it may hint at something more sensual). On the other hand, the Sincere and Polite flirting styles frame the relationship differently. When you are talking to a Sincere or Polite flirt, it is hard to answer the questions, Is it attraction or friendship? and Does she really like me or is she just being nice? The switch of the Sincere or Polite flirt is framing the relationship around closeness or respect, not sexual attraction.

If you think about it in this way, you can see how the switch frames the relationship. It is sort of like a picture frame. It creates boundaries and limits on what is going on. The switch is like a decoder ring that tells you how to interpret the meaning of the whole conversation or, for that matter, a sweet smile or a light touch. In that sense, your particular style of flirting creates a relational frame that makes sense of the words that your new crush is saying. It makes sense of what you are saying for the other person, too. Some styles of flirting make clear that you're interested in something physical and romantic. Other styles of flirting keep that added info under lock and key, because expressing such things goes against your way of doing things. The switch is your main (relational) frame when it comes to attraction.

When you are switched on, you are strongly communicating and highly receptive to messages of attraction—particularly physical attraction. When you are switched off, the signal you send to others is that you are being nice or friendly or you're just uninterested. And when you are switched off, you interpret someone else's messages the same way.

CYBER-FLIRTING

Physical flirts can get really personal really fast when chatting online. They will put a lot of intimate details out there and try to get their partners to do the same.

SEXUAL NEUTRALITY: THE SWITZERLAND OF FLIRTING

The second concept that helps explain the switch is the concept of sexual neutrality. Researchers of human sexuality typically identify sexual neutrality as a state when you are "not consciously thinking about or wanting to have sex, but also not being completely averse to the idea." It is sort of an in-between zone. The idea is that a good sexual partner should be able to steer you out of neutrality to a special, happy place (you fill in the specifics).

However, when I think of sexual neutrality, I think of it as a state of being. Are you normally sexually neutral—not thinking about sex—or are you already in gear—thinking about sex constantly? Some people are sexually neutral by disposition and some are quite the opposite. Remember in the Physical flirting style chapter where I told you about the idea of having sex on the brain? Physical flirts see romantic potential all around them. They believe that people are flirting with them everywhere they go. Physical flirts always have their switch turned on.

Sexual neutrality is a state of being for people whose switch is always in the off position. It isn't that they are against having sex. It isn't that they don't ever feel attracted to people. But sexually neutral people just aren't thinking about sex, the possibility of sex or the sexual tempest that potentially lies beneath people's boring or routine actions. The people who have their switches turned off are just going about their day treating interactions with people at face value. They don't read extra sexual content into conversations. They probably miss most of the more obvious cues of romantic interest given off by others. They simply aren't considering the world this way. And to them, it is OK to be Swiss. They have no problem with their own neutrality—they probably even have a very good reason for being that way.

Sexy Thoughts

Another way to think about sexual neutrality is to consider how often people are consciously thinking about sex. You may have heard that men think about sex every seven seconds. (Research says: This simply isn't true for the vast majority of men or women!) What is true is that there is a huge range in the number of times people think about sex on any given day. Now, you don't have to actively be thinking about sex to interpret a flirtatious glance or conversation as potentially signaling sexual or romantic interest. Thinking about sex may not make you accurate in assessing others' intentions, but it certainly makes sure that you don't miss out.

The FSI Survey gave me an even more to-the-point answer to this question. While you can think about sex in your dreams, in response to advertisements or in the context of a committed relationship, you can also think about sex as a consequence of interactions with real people with whom you are not romantically involved. Thinking about sex in reaction to an everyday interaction with an acquaintance or stranger is a good indicator of whether or not your switch is in the off or on position.

I asked 4,500 people how often they are turned on after interacting with an acquaintance or stranger. Between 35 percent and 45 percent said never or very rarely, which is a good indication that they are switched off. About 10 percent said they felt that way nearly every single day, and another 20 percent experienced it each week. These people are clearly switched on. Of the remaining people, about 20 percent had this experience monthly or so. These folks are in the middle—something that I'm going to get back to later.

What does this all mean?

When our switch is turned on, it is like we are letting our attraction flow out of us without reservation. We are sensitive to and perceptive of attraction from another person flowing back. We are open to feeling turned on sexually by another person (even if it is only in our imagination). The bottom line is whether or not our switch is on or off plays a very important role in whether we are open to communicating our sexual interest and whether or not we accurately perceive (or just imagine) sexual interest emanating from another person.

Relationship Buffer

Another interesting way of thinking about sexual neutrality is considering how being in a relationship affects this state of mind. Being in a relationship heavily dampens sexual desire for new sexual partners—in other words, your switch gets turned off. People who are in relationships, especially happy relationships, don't seek opportunities to cheat and are even less attracted to their opposite-sex friends. Once your switch is in the off position, you are in a state of sexual neutrality. Listen to what two people I interviewed said about how being in a relationship affected their switch:

I'm in a relationship, so that is probably why it's off all the time.
—Xavier, 20 years old

I noticed when I was single and went out with the girls, I was ready to party. Now when I go out, I notice it's just an ugly meat market out there and I want no part of it.
—Nikki, 24 years old

It's not that romantic relationships completely kill your sex drive or make you utterly unresponsive to attraction expressed by other people (if it did kill desire, then there would be no TV show *Cheaters* and the world would be an emptier place). Without a doubt, people cheat and seek attention from other people. However, being in a committed relationship changes the way we interpret interactions with opposite-sex friends and attractive strangers alike. We aren't actively looking for signs of interest because we have shifted gears into sexual neutrality.

This means that the position of your switch can be changed. I won't go so far as to say your switch can be turned off if you are usually on or vice versa. It probably cannot be set in a fundamentally different gear than the way you usually are. However, as a good friend of mine put it, you might not be able to switch completely on or off, but you can put a dimmer on it.

RESEARCH SAYS

When people are in unhappy relationships, they flirt back more in conversations with attractive strangers than people in happy relationships.

EMBRACING THE POSSIBILITY OF ATTRACTION

The third idea is to embrace the possibility of attraction. The switch is the essence of attraction. Everyone, everywhere wants to feel attractive, desirable and interesting. It is not just about wanting to feel attractive, it is about accepting the possibility that someone is attracted to us and would like it if we showed our attraction to them. There are some important reasons we don't feel that way: (1) We don't want to make other people uncomfortable, (2) we don't want to be rejected, and (3) we don't want to be delusional about how attractive we really are. To turn your switch on, you must get into the mind-set that expressing your romantic interest is less an imposition and more a gift. If you don't already believe this is true, I'm going to try to convince you when and why it is.

Why Being Attracted to Someone Matters

Have you ever wondered why it is that beautiful people are treated differently than others? In a classic episode of *30 Rock*, Liz Lemon is dating *Mad Men*'s Don Draper—the terrific Jon Hamm. The joke on this particular *30 Rock* episode is that Jon Hamm's character has no idea that he is exceedingly hand-some. Instead, he thinks that he is exceptional at all kinds of things that he actually really sucks at. He is crap at tennis and is asked by ladies at the tennis club if he gives private lessons. Without question, he is the stupidest doctor in New York City.

Because he is Jon Hamm, everyone wants to be with him and he can get away with nearly anything.

When we think people are attractive, we treat them differently. We believe that attractive people are more interesting, funnier and more socially adept than unattractive people. Crucially, when we are in a conversation with an attractive person, we act in a way that conveys more warmth toward them and confidence in ourselves. We are simply more sociable people when we are talking to attractive partners. As a consequence, we make it *easy* for attractive people to be charming or funny because we treat them like interesting and hilarious people. We ask a bunch of follow-up questions and laugh at their jokes a little harder ("Wow, you are *funny!*"). This gives attractive people the impression that they are funny, interesting and important. But they are not necessarily that way inherently. They *feel* that way because of the way we act.

The point that I am trying to make is this: deep down everyone knows that being attracted to someone tends to make us behave in a more attractive manner. This may be a consequence of the conscious attempt to put our best foot forward. It may be just a happy side effect of the heady feeling of attraction. In either case, giving in to our feelings of attraction makes us warmer and more engaged during a conversation. But what about the other way around—thinking that someone is attracted to us?

Why Perceiving Attraction Matters

Easily one of the top-rated, most important qualities we seek in other people is that they are attracted to us. It tops nearly every list when it is included as an option. Wanting mutual attraction in a romantic relationship is so obvious, in fact, that a lot of times people don't even bother to mention it as a desirable quality. People will rattle off their favorite features in a romantic partner: sense of humor, warmth, being a good kisser and intelligence, but will totally forget a big one: she is attracted to me. When that's brought to their attention, people think, *Well, duh, isn't that a given?*

No, it isn't a given! Instead, we work hard when we are flirting and dating to get our crush to like us. Whether he seems to be attracted to us really matters when it comes to how we behave and how we feel about ourselves. It matters when it comes to what we think and feel about our crush, too. Knowing someone is attracted to us seriously influences how we evaluate his potential as both a hookup and a spouse. This means that the perception that someone likes us makes a big difference in how we feel and how we treat others.

Topping 10

The discovery of interest from another person changes her from an 8 to a 10. The discovery of *mutual* attraction makes her seem like she'd be a good person to take home tonight, a good catch to start dating and just maybe someone you'd like to marry. Once you believe that someone is attracted to you, you change, too. You begin to share more about yourself. You begin to actively seek common interests and similarities with her. You start feeling better and better about everything in general and that person in particular. So why don't we go around thinking, *Everyone is totally into me* all the time?

Those people *do* exist and they are called narcissists. People don't like narcissists. Even though we might be initially impressed by their strong self-confidence and clearheaded self-assurance, it starts to wear thin as soon as we get past the get-to-know-ya stage. Instead, we prefer people who have a pretty accurate estimate of how attractive they are and how much people like them.

On the other hand, there are lots of people who drastically underestimate their own appeal. They might have low self-esteem or they may not want to draw attention to themselves, either physically or socially. They may be particularly worried about being disappointed if their own self-image turns out to be false. So what does all this have to do with flirting?

Perceiving Attraction and Flirting

Let's say that someone is flirting with you. For whatever reason, she is making it clear she is interested in you. In knowing and accepting this information, you start acting in a more confident and more charming way. One man I interviewed described it this way, "If my switch were off, I would feel less attention. I would give less attention, too." If your switch were totally off and you never perceived flirting, not only would you miss out on every possible relationship or love interest that came your way, you'd miss out on a lot of potential attention. Consequently, you'd give a lot less attention than you would if you simply acknowledged that you were considered attractive in the eyes of another person.

When I asked her why her flirting switch was turned on, one young woman I interviewed told me: "I guess it makes me happy. I see flirting and friendliness as being really close together. I'm an open and happy person and I guess I like flirting. But it's not like I'm always looking for a guy. For me, flirting makes me feel happy." Getting caught up in the feeling of perceiving attraction from another person makes us feel good. It is reassuring and enjoyable. To experience this, we have to be open to the possibility that others are romantically interested in us.

I want to be very clear; it isn't that flirting is always a pathway to sex, intimacy or romance. It isn't that it is always done for selfish gain or for a purely egocentric boost. Without question, flirting is tied to giving and receiving attention and attraction. This is exactly what it feels like to turn your switch on. When your switch is on, you express the interest you feel and you are open to the interest that others express toward you.

WHY SHOWING ATTENTION MATTERS

If you can accept that flirting doesn't just have to be about romance, then you can begin to see that flirting is also a way of expressing your interest in others. A young man I interviewed told me that his switch was definitely on. When I asked why, he said, "I think flirting is borderline being friendly. It's easy to cross over into flirting when you're already being nice." A woman agreed: "It's kinda fun. People like you more if you're flirting with them, so it makes you more likable. Being flirtatious with someone can make you more interesting in their eyes." In showing our interest in other people, we draw attention to ourselves. Flirting enables us to elicit that attention from other people.

One friend of mine told me he used to flirt with the older ladies at his church. Every week he'd walk up to them after church to compliment them on their dresses and attempt to charm them. "Of course, it was all completely innocent," he told me. "My wife was there the whole time. For me, it was just a way of showing them that I cared. I guess I wanted to let them know that I noticed them." Flirting is acknowledgment and it's validation. It says, "I see you there looking good." It also sends the message, "Now see me" or "Look for me later." Not necessarily for anything other than a little more innocent, affectionate communication of interest.

REASONS TO SWITCH OFF

When I interviewed people about their own flirting switch, I found a lot of people who were always on and a lot who were always off. There were two very common reasons that people kept their switch off: flirting is an imposition or they don't trust people who flirt for no reason. These are both important positions to consider.

Is flirting an imposition?

The first point of view is fascinating to me because it makes so much sense and applies to so many situations. Essentially, these people were telling me that flirting obliges someone to respond to you. No doubt, this *may* be a problem. In the case of flirting with someone at work, it could get you fired because flirting may be construed as a form of sexual harassment. Therefore, isn't flirting an imposition on another person's privacy or personal bubble?

There are two sides to this coin. On one side, you respect the other person's privacy and always maintain an appropriate distance. On the other, you privilege your own desire to express attraction. This two-sided dilemma is intensely felt by people who are trying to muster up the courage to ask someone out. They don't want to put pressure on the person they're interested in if that person doesn't reciprocate their interest, so they err on the side of privacy, caution and indirectness. They typically beat around the bush when asking someone for a date.

When thinking about it this way, people with more direct styles of flirting tend to put their own needs over those of the other person, even at risk of making the other person uncomfortable. And this is not always a good thing. As one young man told me in explaining why his switch was off: "I just prefer to err on the safe side." Not expressing your romantic interest is undoubtedly safer for both you and the other person. In some places, like work, it may be absolutely necessary to keep your job.

I Don't Trust the Player

The other reason people keep their switch in the off position is that they want to protect themselves from unwanted sexual advances because they mistrust other people's motives. A college-aged female explained it to me this way: "What would it be like to have my switch turned on? I think I'd have to be a completely different person. I'd have to look at social interactions completely differently. If your switch were on, you'd have to look at social interactions basically from a sexual standpoint. If I were switched on, I would think, *What are their motives?* Whereas now I'm looking at it from a different point of view. I am like, *What interests me about what they are saying?* What she means is that by framing the conversation around a particular topic and ignoring what might be the other person's sexual or romantic intentions, you keep your switch off. You keep your distance and respect his privacy, but you also might miss out on cues indicating that he is having more than a polite or friendly conversation with you.

Being switched on makes you more aware of a person's sexual motives, which may be a bit uncomfortable for you. For women, particularly, doubting the honesty or purity of men's motives is a major concern when it comes to flirting (and for good reason). However, being switched off isn't just about mistrusting his motives; it is about whether you are paying attention to what is being said in an interaction and whether it might be flirting. People whose switch is off prefer to keep conversations on topic and about the things they are clearly about. As a consequence, they tend to be rather literal about conveying and interpreting interest. What this means is that they completely ignore many hints or fail to respond to them.

SWITCH ON

Drawing from my interviews with people about their own switch, I'd like to give you a quick rundown about what it feels like to have your switch turned on and turned off. Here are some quotes from men and women I interviewed. Their names have been changed, but these quotes are real. The first group are those who would describe their switch as turned on.

What does it feel like to have your switch on?

- **"Flirting is a way of socializing for me. If it's off, I'm not being as social."** —Eric, 20 years old, Physical and Traditional flirting style
- **"It's like I've got a lot of personality, I guess. It makes me feel more lively. If my switch were off, it'd be like a rainy day in a person."** —Maya, 24 years old, Playful and Physical flirting style
- **"I'm always playful with people, even ones I don't know. I grew up around girls, so I always kind of know how to act around them. I've been trained. [laughs]"** —Logan, 30 years old, Playful and Sincere flirting style
- **"I flirt a lot, but it's not so much that I flirt with everyone I see. Flirting makes me feel attractive, and I feel that is true for everyone. Flirting makes you comfortable. You feel better about yourself."** —Marcia, 37 years old, Playful flirting style

What are the good parts of being on?

- **"I am a waiter, so it helps to have my switch on. I compliment everyone, unless it's a table full of dudes. It's part of the job. Some of it isn't flirting; it's being extra nice."** —Carl, 25 years old, Playful flirting style
- **"I'm usually really talkative at a bar, always laughing, so maybe that attracts guys. I don't really shove guys**

off, as some girls do when they don't want to talk to
a guy. I'm open to talking to anyone. Maybe that makes
me attractive." —Anna, 40 years old, Sincere flirting style
- "Not that I flirt to make myself feel better, but I feel
like it comes with the territory. It is something that
I can do if I *need* to." —Mauricio, 28 years old, Physical
and Traditional flirting style

What are the drawbacks?

- "I'm just kinda known to be flirtatious with guys and
stuff like that. A lot of my guy friends have said that
and it drives my boyfriend insane." —Robin, 21 years old,
Physical and Traditional flirting style
- "Sometimes I feel like I can't talk to someone without
flirting or without somebody getting the wrong idea.
Even when I'm working in a group, I can see that
there's flirting going on." —Kathryn, 23 years old,
Physical flirting style
- "Oh my God, I've bombed so many times. Should
I just pick one? [laughs]" —Marcus, 29 years old, Playful
flirting style

There are a couple of key things about these quotes that I want
to emphasize. Having your switch on isn't a choice, exactly. It
certainly has consequences, but it isn't something that a person
just does or doesn't do at will or with conscious intent. A lot of
people with their switch on just accept being that way. They
understand that it gives them benefits of attention, confidence
and being social. But they also know that being switched on

isn't without consequences. A person with her switch on also runs into the problem of someone getting the wrong idea or getting rejected. She is just more comfortable with the feeling of being switched on—both the good and the bad that come with it. People switched on will often use it to their advantage. They might flirt to feel better or get the attention they want. The Playful flirting style is particularly tied into being switched on that way. Flirting is a means to an end.

SWITCH OFF

What does it feel like to have your switch off?

- **"I'm really comfortable around people and I like talking to new people. I am the guy who is always the perfect gentlemen to my friends' girlfriends. I think that's a major advantage. I'm not a threat; I'm I good friend."** —Adam, 47 years old, Sincere and Traditional flirting style
- **"Generally it is off because when I go out, I'm not trying to meet anyone special. Mostly because I think it's pointless. It's not like you ever have a meaningful conversation with someone at a bar. That's the real way to get to know someone."** —Kelly, 36 years old, Traditional flirting style
- **"I feel that anytime I can get a girl comfortable enough to talk about herself and share personal information, then it is successful. It isn't about flirting, it is about being comfortable with people."** —Raj, 23 years old, Polite and Sincere flirting style

What are the good parts of being off?

- "When I go out with my friends, I mainly talk to the people I came with. It is important to me that nobody gets left out because other guys are trying to pick up on some chick." —Russell, 32 years old, Polite and Traditional flirting style
- "I'm really outgoing and friendly, but flirting is rarely on my mind. That means I can be comfortable with guys in conversations where there might be something else going on. A lot of times I'll just think a guy is being friendly and then later realize he might have been flirting. From my perspective, that is a good thing. Being switched off means I wasn't overly nervous or trying to impress anyone—I was just being myself." —Michelle, 25 years old, Playful and Sincere flirting style

What are the drawbacks?

- "The downside? It takes a lot of effort for me to try to flirt with someone. I need a pep talk. [laughs]" —Ryan, 24 years old, Polite flirting style
- "In most situations, I'm not open to being hit on. If I'm in a social outing, then I'd probably notice. But if I were in a grocery store and somebody was flirting with me, I wouldn't even notice. I wouldn't be aware that's what they were doing."—Jamie, 36 years old, Sincere flirting style
- "I'd like to be more aware that it's happening, when it's happening. I've found myself in situations where after I left the conversation, I'm like, 'He was totally flirting

with me!' and 'He was good-looking! How could I have missed it?'" —Jada, 42 years old, Polite flirting style

Here are a couple of things to keep in mind about those who have switches that are generally off. Being switched off is partly a mind-set, but it is also part of a self-image. People who are off can be quite friendly and social, but they just aren't paying attention to the attraction coming back at them. Sometimes they are making a conscious choice not to put themselves out there, because they think it is needy or inappropriate. Some flirts in the off position are very charming people, but they pride themselves in playing it safe around their friends' girlfriends or boyfriends or maybe just around other people in general. You might be tempted to say that people who are in the off position aren't good at flirting. This is simply not true. It is probably more accurate to say they just aren't using their natural flirting style and innate abilities to actively attempt to flirt.

USE THE SWITCH TO FLIRT SMARTER

As I've said, there is no one right way to flirt. Certain flirting styles are associated with having your switch on; people with these styles tend to send a more overt message of attraction and pick up potential interest in others. Other styles are associated with having their switch off; people with these styles tend to flirt less obviously or aggressively and don't always pick up on the signals that others send out.

The beauty of the switch is that all flirting styles can use the power of the switch to flirt more effectively, to use what they've got to their advantage. Step one to doing this is getting to know whether your switch is on or off, then figuring out how to loosen it up.

KNOW YOUR SWITCH

Being aware of how we communicate romantic interest and attraction gives us insight into how our own flirting style may not always work for us. If you're not "lucky in love" or your flirting style doesn't produce the desired results, you should know that flirting is inherently complicated and most people struggle with the same frustration you do. This can manifest itself in different ways—you might have trouble attracting your crushes, you might not recognize when someone has a crush on you or you might have no problem getting attention, but you always get it from the "wrong" people—those who aren't looking for the same thing you are.

The good news is that because all people are a mix of styles, you can tailor your flirting style to suit your needs. Emphasize the aspects of your flirting style that match your relationship goals and tone down the styles that do not. It is easier to emphasize or minimize parts of our behavior that are already inherent to our nature, than to change them completely.

The switch is an important part of this because it changes the message you send out and the way you receive messages. If you are very high on the Playful or Physical styles, then you are probably switched on. If you are very high on the Polite style or if you are a woman and high on the Traditional style, then you are likely switched off. If those quick rules of thumb aren't enough and you still aren't sure whether you are switched on or off, answer each of these four questions for yourself:

1. Do other people often think you are flirting, even when you don't mean to?
2. Do you find yourself considering how sexually attractive or exciting opposite-sex strangers are when first meeting them?
3. Do you often intentionally put the brakes on showing your romantic interest in other people for their sake (or for your own)?
4. When you meet new people, are you more likely to consider whether they'd make a good friend or a good lover?

If you said *yes* to questions 1 and 2, *no* to question 3 and *good lover* to question 4, then chances are your switch is on. If you said *no* to questions 1 and 2, *yes* to 3 and *good friend* to 4, then chances are your switch is off. If you answered some combination of the above questions, then your switch is somewhere in the middle. For you, both of the next sections might apply. You also have an advantage because you are already aware that your internal attraction needs to be appropriate to the context and managed.

Now that you know whether your switch is on or off, I'm going to help you figure out how to turn it up or down to get the results you want when you flirt. Switching on isn't always the best thing, nor is switching off. Based on the information you've read in this chapter, you should have a good sense of when you need to be more on and when you need to be more off. You can use the following exercises to dim or brighten your own switch as needed.

SWITCHING ON

If you are switched off, you know how hard it is to flirt on command. You don't have a lot of practice putting yourself out there or approaching attractive members of the opposite sex. However, there are things you can do that can help you get started turning your switch on. Below is a list of tips and exercises that can help you get your switch loosened up.

1. **Practice feeling interested.** There are a lot of people who think flirting is a skill that people have either got or not. They also don't realize that those who have the most success in flirting also have most of the failures. You've got to be rejected to be accepted. Now I'm not going to throw you to the wolves and just say, "Go do it." Instead, you need to practice something much simpler: you must practice feeling interested. You can do this by accepting and being aware of feeling attracted or interested in someone and letting it affect how you act. One way to practice this is to accept feeling interested in people you don't know and probably won't see again. When you interact with a cashier, waiter or store clerk who is attractive

to you, take a moment and pause. Smile to yourself and recognize that you are attracted to her. Then, for the rest of your meal, sale or interaction, keep that recognition in your head. Embrace feeling interested. This does not mean that you tell her or *try* to flirt with her. (For goodness sake, do not try out some awful pickup line.) Instead, I want you to be able to know what that feeling is like and observe how it influences your actions. Practice feeling interested and being comfortable with that feeling.

2. **Adopt an open mind-set.** As children, we were much more comfortable playing make-believe (thank you, Mr. Rogers). We could pretend we were riding a motorcycle while on a tricycle. Pretending is imaginative and it changes our mind-set about ourselves and those around us. To begin to flip your switch on, you may have to do the same thing. You need to start actively seeking signs of attraction. Even if you think this is only a bit of make-believe. This self-doubt is your off switch talking. Accept the possibility that someone you know is interested in you. Once you have identified that person, the next time you talk to him try imagining that he is really interested in you. Accept that interest as if it were completely true. Be open to it. The consequences of this activity should be revelatory. How does that knowledge change you? What does it feel like to believe it? Once you can convince yourself through imagining his interest, you will be much more alert to what it feels like

when it actually happens. You might have the happy consequence of finding a partner whose flirting style is more Polite and appropriate, that is, switched off.

3. **Know the context.** One insight that people with their switch on can give those who are off is that context matters. Here is a choice quote about whether or not a guy is flirting or just being friendly when he is talking to a girl at a bar: "If you're talking to a stranger, then it's probably flirting. I mean, not too many guys at the bar talk to strange women to form a friendship." Often this little insight is lost on women with their switch off. They are paying close attention to the topic of the conversation, worried about whether or not he is just being friendly, or they are simply oblivious to his cues. It is best in such a place to believe that it is *always* flirting. More importantly, you need to remember and act on that knowledge the moment it happens. In other places, like the grocery store or your workplace, this rule does not apply. When you are at a bar or a club, it is simply flirting, plain and simple. Practice being aware of how your surroundings influence the meaning of interactions—the context frames the relationship!

4. **Watch carefully.** Research tells us that men don't know that they approach women who signal them to come over. Women don't know they are signaling the men who are approaching them. There is a long history of research that shows that people are just not particularly aware of their own nonverbal actions and others' responses to those actions. To get your switch

loosened up, start being a people watcher. Students of nonverbal communication begin to see nonverbal behavior all around them that they tended not to notice before. You must do that with flirting. Notice how women flirt with men. Notice how men flirt with women. Watch couples interact at a bar and try to guess if they are on a first date or already in a relationship. Practice being more aware of flirting in general. People who are switched off lack awareness. They often complain that they are oblivious to the interest of others. By noticing it more in others, you will be less oblivious when it happens to you.

5. **Pump yourself up.** In the stories I told at the beginning of the flirting styles chapters, you may have noticed that people with certain flirting styles were more likely to preparty and get pumped up before going out. Getting pumped up doesn't have to mean taking tequila shots with friends before hitting the bar. It means pumping yourself up mentally by telling yourself, "I look really *good* today." Recognize that the way you dress matters when it comes to first impressions and dress accordingly. But the most important thing is to adopt the mind-set that people want to flirt with you. Begin to believe that they want you. One of the most exciting sexual fantasies you can entertain is the belief that other people want you. That fantasy is a good way to start adjusting your switch. If you don't feel comfortable believing that people want you, then your fantasy can be

"I have a dazzling personality" or "I own this party. This is my place." The bottom line is to get pumped up. Do what it takes to make yourself believe that other people are interested in getting to know you better.

6. **Remember your other strengths.** A recent study on women who initiate romantic relationships found that assertive women tend to achieve more success and control in other aspects of their lives. By having women write down and think about the things they were good at in their lives, like their studies or careers, researchers found that women were more willing to put effort into controlling their dating destiny. I believe this is probably true for men as well. Remembering the things you are good at not only makes you feel confident, but it gives you some good talking points when you are presenting yourself to someone new. Let's face it: flirting is about some honest self-promotion, too.

By practicing these tips, you will get to know what it feels like to turn your switch on. When your switch is on, you express the interest you genuinely feel and you are open to the interest that others express to you.

Remember, flirting isn't about sex or being promiscuous. It is about perceiving interest in another person for all their distinctive qualities—physical, mental, spiritual and otherwise—and giving that attention right back to them. People love seeing that other people are aware of their good qualities.

SWITCHING OFF

The challenges of flirts with their switch in the on position are utterly different than those whose switch is turned off. Rather than a lack of sexual thoughts or a lack of willingness to be available, switched-on flirts are quite attuned to the attraction and interest communicated all around them. My advice about turning it down a notch focuses on things that people who are switched on may not be aware of or are not paying attention to when they flirt. Being always switched on has its drawbacks, and knowing how to control intense feelings of attraction is definitely beneficial.

1. **People have a right to their bubble.** Everyone has a personal space bubble that extends about 1½ feet around them on all sides. In some cultures that bubble is bigger, and in some cultures it is smaller. (The American bubble is a bit bigger than that in Southern Europe and Latin America.) However, people generally prefer to keep their bubble free of strangers, whether on an airplane or at their job. People who are switched on touch others freely and are a type of space invader. Even at clubs or bars, where people are open to being flirted with, one of the top complaints voiced by women is that guys may invade their personal space or are too touchy and grabby. Touch is one of our most powerful ways to communicate because it expresses both love and hate, both affection

and domination. Those who are switched on need to develop a better awareness of other people's personal bubble and remember that even a little touch can be an unwelcome space invasion.

2. **Location, location, location.** Consider the old saying: There is a time and a place for everything. This is a good lesson for those who are switched on. There is no problem with being friendly, laughing and enjoying the company of others. This is true pretty much no matter where you are. Whether or not you take it too far, however, depends on where you are. There is a very different level of politeness expected in the office than at the club. Finding out where you easily keep your switch off is a good way to learn how to control it. One young woman whose switch was usually on told me, "The only time I'd say it's off is when I'm around my family. I'm more conscious of how I talk when I'm around my family." This is sort of like using your inside voice. Sometimes you need to keep that sexual and physical energy out of the picture, just as you would if you were around your mother or father. If you need a little extra help doing this, imagine that your grandmother were there, watching you. The feeling that you might want to restrict your behavior is a good way to learn what it feels like to turn down your bright lights.

3. **Stepping on toes.** Part of the difficulty for people who are switched on is that they value attracting the attention of others and expressing their own interest,

sometimes over the needs of others. It is no surprise that many naturally switched-on flirts had issues with their partner feeling jealous. Each of us has a choice about how we interact. Just because you *could* capture the attention of the hot guy/girl at the office doesn't mean you *should*. It is not only disrespectful to that person's partner, it confuses the working relationship. Not stepping on toes doesn't just apply to men and women already in a relationship. It applies to everyone. Part of switching off means recognizing that many people don't want your compliment, don't want your attention and would like to keep things as professional as possible.

4. **Stay sober.** It probably comes as no surprise that the hookup culture is fueled by alcohol. A lot of hookups occur under the influence, and in the vast majority of hookups people regretted the most, alcohol was involved. If this is something you can relate to, then it might be time to think about developing your flirting style without a drink in your hand. Staying sober is a good way to avoid getting into a bad situation (or putting someone else in a bad situation), but it is also a good way to cultivate a bit of self-reflection when it comes to flirting. Take one night to go out and not drink. Watch how your own interpretation of people changes. What are you uncomfortable doing sober that you would be willing to do if you had several shots of Goldschläger? By

watching how other people act and noticing the way they look under the influence, you can gain some insight about how you probably look, too. There is nothing like realizing the look of foolishness to make you want to avoid it.

5. **What sort of attention are you seeking?** There is a difference between being interested in someone as a person and being interested in someone solely to attract attention. Flirts who are chronically switched on have the misconception that missing out on attention is unthinkable. One young man said, "If I were off, I wouldn't be as interesting." This kind of thinking—that being off means you're being rude, boring or downbeat—simply is not true. You need to recognize that not all attention is good attention. People who seek attention above all else are often much more interested in casual sex, rather than sex in the context of a relationship. This isn't a problem in itself, but it may not match your relationship goals. Sometimes it is a good idea to avoid garnering potential attention because not everyone is someone you want attention from. Furthermore, attention seekers are fun at a party, but they can also be a drag when they drain attention from everyone else. Getting attention from other people can become like a drug that you don't want to stop taking. Practice accepting what it feels like not to seek it out.

BE FLEXIBLE

The last key to being able to control your switch is to recognize when to turn it on and when to turn it off. Like mood lighting or a dimmer switch, you will want to be able to freely turn on and off your bright light. Good communicators are flexible. They recognize that context matters and that they can change how they act depending on what is called for in a particular situation. Flirting works the same way. When you know how the switch feels, and what it takes to kick it up a notch or tone it down, you'll be able to use your switch when you need it most.

Chapter Eight

PERCEPTIONS AND MISPERCEPTIONS

As promised in Chapter 7, "The Switch," we now return to the big question: How do I know if someone is flirting with me? As I mentioned before, with this question comes several other important questions: Is he interested in me romantically or is he just being nice? Is she flirting because she likes me, or is it because she is trying to make someone else jealous? Is he interested in developing a romantic relationship or just looking for someone for tonight? What you are trying to figure out is whether he is interested in you in the way you want to be wanted and the way you want him back.

Knowing that a person is interested in you is an important first step for all romantic relationships and getting it wrong could set you off in the wrong direction. If you incorrectly think some-one is interested in you, then you are wasting time talking to the wrong person when you could be talking to Mr. or Ms. Right. Worse yet, by talking to someone who isn't interested, you are opening yourself up for rejection and embarrassment.

To answer these challenging questions, I've drawn from cutting-edge research to pinpoint the nine rules of flirting:

Rule #1: Flirting is hard to accurately distinguish from being friendly or nice.

Rule #2: Men are easier to read than women because men are obvious and women are inscrutable.

Rule #3: Men generally think women are more romantically interested than they really are.

Rule #4: Body language is your best bet for telling if someone is interested.

Rule #5: The fear of rejection or looking bad makes flirting less direct.

Rule #6: Flirting is *not* just about sexual or romantic attraction.

Rule #7: Women are in control of the interaction.

Rule #8: You can be clearer.

Rule #9: You can be more accurate.

RULE #1 Flirting is hard to accurately distinguish from being friendly or nice.

I'm guessing Rule #1 comes as no surprise to anyone. You are probably swamped by popular advice about what to look for when flirting, but still not so sure that you know it when you see it. What you might not know is that accurately judging flirting is as hard for regular people as it is for researchers who do this sort of thing for a living (which is the best job in the world, by the way). There are three reasons accurately detecting flirting is so hard: (1) Flirting looks a lot like being outgoing; (2) behaviors that convey romantic interest are harder to detect than everyday emotions, like happiness and sadness; and (3) romantic interest and being nice look very similar.

Flirting and Friendly

Friendly and outgoing people are often mistaken for being flirtatious. It is also true that when you are interested in someone, you begin to act in a more friendly and outgoing way. This means that some body language that seems flirtatious actually indicates that someone is just being friendly. It also means that body language that may just seem friendly is actually flirtatious. As a consequence, people often mistake friendliness for flirting and vice versa.

Consider this research study: when people are asked to generate two lists—one that specifies all the nonverbal signs showing that someone is interested in having a conversation, and a second that specifies all the signs showing that a person is interested in dating—the two lists look remarkably similar. Asking questions, making eye contact, nodding and smiling are on both lists. Even more confusing, some of the signs that indicate a lack of interest also are signs of romantic interest, such as being vague or subtle or making small talk. Some people with flirting styles like the Sincere style act friendly for the purpose of discovering and communicating romantic interest. Essentially, they are being *friendly to flirt*. Small wonder this is so difficult.

Romantic Interest Is Hard to Detect

A recent exciting study by Dr. Coreen Farris and her colleagues explored the issue of distinguishing flirting from friendliness head-on. Dr. Farris had men and women look at photos of women who were friendly, sexually interested, sad or rejecting. Participants in her study had to guess what they thought each woman was thinking or feeling. Essentially, Dr. Farris wanted to know this: When a woman shows that she is sexually interested, can people accurately interpret it? Dr. Farris's conclusion was that it is much easier to tell when a woman is being friendly than when she is expressing sexual interest. Not only is flirting hard to distinguish from just being friendly, it is easier to accurately tell if a woman is *not* interested than to accurately tell if she *is* sexually interested! To put it another way, you are better able to tell if she wants to end the conversation than if she wants to continue the conversation because she likes you.

Look for the Signs

Another popular way of thinking about flirting is to look for the nonverbal signs: a light touch on the hand, deep eye contact, primping hair and smiling. The problem with this approach isn't that it isn't accurate—true, all those behaviors *are* flirting. The problem is that there are lots of other things going on when two people are trying to make a connection. In one of the most advanced studies of nonverbal signs and flirting, Karl Grammer and his research team broke down all the nonverbal signs of flirting in one-on-one conversations between 90 men and women. What they found is that if a woman is interested in a guy, she shows 16 nonverbal signs per minute, but if she isn't interested she still sends 11 signs!

RULE #2 Men are easier to read than women because men are obvious and women are inscrutable.

First things first: it is not the case that all women are inscrutable and all men are obvious. Some people display their romantic desire and attraction like a vacancy sign on a lonely highway. Other people are much more subtle: nothing short of a deathbed confession or an accidentally intercepted secret diary would let you in on their feelings. In fact, when the most transparent men and the most transparent women are compared, men and women are both equally readable. Really obvious men and really obvious women are both really obvious. But after you get past those blinking headlight types, it turns out that men are generally much more transparent when they show their romantic attraction than women are.

There are a couple of good reasons for this. First, it is traditionally the man's job to pursue. Even if men aren't Traditional flirts, they are expected to put the moves on women. A man has to signal his interest fast and clearly so that a woman knows he is interested. Women, especially very Traditional women, will act coy and display subtle, noncommittal and even ambivalent signs of interest. Now why would women do this?

The Consequences of Obviousness

Women have a lot more to lose by being obvious. The double standard in our society says that guys who are hungry for sex and show it willingly are good and manly. But women who are hungry for sex and show it willingly are bad, desperate and slutty. Therefore, women, even those who are very interested in a guy, learn to hide it, disguise it and suppress it. They don't want the painful hand of judgment coming down and smacking them across the ego.

The last (good) reason that women are hard to read when it comes to romance is that women need to take some time to make sure a guy isn't lying. The most effective pickup artists out there are also high-caliber liars. They are totally willing to use deception, exaggerate doing and having things they really don't do or really don't have. They will make all kinds of promises to seduce a woman. Being the more prudent sex, a woman needs to take her time in figuring out whether a guy really is who he says he is.

Speed-Dating Confirmation

Amazingly, there is a study of people at a speed-dating event that confirmed all this. Dr. Skyler Place and his colleagues videotaped people at a speed-dating gathering and matched up the videos with whether or not each of the participants said they'd go out on a date with their conversational partner. Dr. Place had a real-world measure of romantic interest: Would you go on a date with this person: *yes* or *no?* Knowing whether each person said *yes* or *no* after any given videotaped interaction, he showed these videos to people who were strangers to both of the conversationalists. They were then asked, "Was the person in the video interested: *yes* or *no?*"

Dr. Place found that when strangers tried to guess whether or not women were interested, their guesses were barely better than 50/50. The strangers might as well have flipped a coin and been just as accurate! It wasn't just men who were inaccurate; women were no better at judging other women's interest than men were. The women at this speed-dating event were simply inscrutable!

The men at the speed-dating event were a totally different story. Strangers could tell with amazing accuracy whether a guy was interested in dating the woman he was talking to. With a guy, you can just tell. He doesn't have to buy a drink, approach a woman, drop a pickup line or ask for a dance. He shows how interested he is in a three-minute conversation with a woman he has just met!

RULE #3 Men generally think women are more romantically interested than they really are.

Again, this rule will come as no surprise to women who have tried to let a guy down easily because he got the wrong idea, or for women who are stunned that a guy could not have known she was interested. The question is this: Why is this true?

Research says

Twenty-six percent of women have had men mistake their friendliness for flirting.

Why?

One of the most consistent findings in flirting research is that men mistake a woman's friendliness for seductiveness or flirtatiousness. There are a couple of possible explanations for this phenomenon. One explanation is that men engage in more wishful thinking than women do. As I mentioned in Chapter 7, "The Switch," we like attractive people and want them to like us, too. In hopes of finding clues of attraction, or in an attempt to emphasize the flirtatiousness and diminish the friendliness he does see, a man will perceive a woman as being more flirtatious than the woman really is.

The second possibility is that men do this in response to inscrutable women. Men are stuck in this situation: they can't tell whether women are interested, but they don't want to miss out on being with a woman who already likes them. Therefore, men have an internal mechanism that exaggerates women's attraction. The theory is that it would be simply too costly to miss out on a potential romantic partner, so men evolved this overestimating bias. Another way to say this is that men assume sexual interest because it's better to be wrong and suffer a little rejection and embarrassment than to miss out on being with a woman who is interested and available.

The third possibility is that men are simply less effective decoders of nonverbal communication than women are. This explanation means that men are less adept at reading nonverbal emotions in general, so when it comes to reading signs of interest, they get easily confused.

The bottom line is that all three of the above explanations have good supporting research. Whatever the reason, Rule #3 is true.

RULE #4 Body language is your best bet for telling if someone is interested.

As if they were studying the mating rituals of the blue baboon or the Eastern U.S. mockingbird, researchers of human courtship have been convinced for many years that they can nail down the exact signs of sexual attraction. Unlike our primate cousins who will point to their genitalia with great relish when they're in heat, human beings are fortunately more self-conscious and concerned with how their actions will be perceived by others, so we don't clearly signal our romantic interest. Undaunted, researchers haven't given up trying to figure out what the signs of attraction are. There are some exceptional studies that can help figure this all out.

RESEARCH SAYS

If someone is obviously flirting with you, there is a better chance he is interested in sex than love. If someone is flirting in subtle ways, so you can't tell how interested she is, then she is more interested in love than sex.

Frequency versus Obviousness

I was on a radio show and the host asked me, "What are the signs that a woman is interested in a man?" When I started listing the signs, the host interrupted and asked rather crassly, "What if she spreads her legs apart? Isn't that a sign?" Without missing a beat, I replied, "It means you are probably at a strip club and not on a date." This little exchange told me something important about the way that people think about nonverbal signs of attraction.

I believe that TV shows and movies, strip clubs and sexually explicit advertising have totally screwed up our perception of what flirting is (particularly men's perception). Every week a new commercial will come out that has scantily clad, gorgeous women obviously showing their uncontrollable interest in a guy (probably because of his choice of light beer or cheap body spray). Movies are no better. Usually, the male and female protagonists so clearly show the audience how much they want each other, we have no choice but to believe them. As a consequence, we believe that these signs of attraction are just as clear in real life. The truth is, unless you are at a strip club, you will probably never see a woman act like this. It simply isn't realistic.

What does happen is that women and men will very subtly, very briefly and unintentionally flash signs of interest in a matter of milliseconds. These are called micro-expressions. These little signs have two important qualities—they are rare and they are powerful indicators of attraction. However, there are a whole host of other signs that are pretty good indicators that a woman is agreeable to the conversation, but do not clearly distinguish whether she is interested in romance or just being friendly. To give you a rundown of the results of decades of work on the nonverbal signs of attraction, I've placed flirting signals into three categories: (1) ultrarare and quite obvious, (2) somewhat frequent and relatively hard to see, and (3) frequent, easy to see, but inconsistently related to attraction and only attraction.

ULTRARARE AND QUITE OBVIOUS

One of the trailblazing researchers on flirting, Dr. Monica Moore, did outstanding work on the signs of attraction. In her work, she went to all kinds of places and documented how women signal that they are available to be approached by men. Although she did not identify any *one* particular behavior that was a sure-fire sign of availability and interest by women, she generated several terrific lists of possible signs.

Here are four signs that fit the rare and obvious category: lick lips, hike up skirt (then pull it down), coy smile (smile, look away, then cover mouth) and hair primp (like bobbing hair with her hands, 1950s-style). These four signs happened very rarely, but clearly conveyed interest in being approached by a guy. If you are male and you see these signs, you should probably do something about it. A man perceives each of these four signs as obvious and positive signs that a woman is interested in him. That means, if you want a man to approach you, these four are clear ways to signal him to do just that.

Although there hasn't been research on this, I imagine that there are even more rare indicators that women are interested: licking or sucking on her fingers, sitting on a man's lap, stroking his leg or body, kissing him anywhere, and bending over in provocative ways. These signs have probably never been studied because they so rarely happen in everyday life with everyday people (despite how often they happen in TV shows and commercials). Sorry, gentlemen. This isn't going to happen for most of you. Unless you are a movie star or otherwise famous, it is extremely unlikely that any woman will approach you in this way.

SOMEWHAT FREQUENT AND RELATIVELY HARD TO SEE

Next, we get to the signs that are much more likely to happen, but might go unnoticed. The biggest type of behavior in this category is gazing, looking and making eye contact. Everyone seems to agree that eye contact is practically a requirement for men to approach women. Women know that women do it and men know that women do it—even if they won't admit to doing it themselves. This sign of romantic interest takes two to tango. Men who are interested in talking to or meeting someone new will often scan the room to look for women who catch their eye. Women often invite a man to approach by giving him a short glance and then looking away. Now a guy may not always realize that this is happening. He thinks he is doing the approaching; he doesn't consciously know that he is accepting an invitation. Even more interesting, women often don't know they are doing it, either. This makes glances and eye contact fit into the relatively hard to see category. To get the conversation started by making a guy approach her, a woman has to get caught looking. It often helps to do it more than once (see above regarding guys' lack of nonverbal decoding skills).

There are two more little things a woman can do to help get a guy to approach her: she can walk near or talk loudly to get his attention. The near walking is a great little strategy. It can take two forms. The first form is a woman walking by strutting or swaying. As long as her walk is in his line of sight, it will get his eyes following her as she goes. I mean how many famous songs are there about men watching women walk? (My personal favorite is "Girl from Ipanema.") The other strategy she could try is occupying his space so he is bound to bump into her. This, of course, is all planned.

These strategies are relatively uncommon, and also have the unfortunate side effect of generating attention from other guys in her general proximity that she has no interest in. Nonetheless, there is good evidence that these things work. Although attractive women are approached more in general, a woman who signals her availability using these strategies gets approached the most regardless of how attractive she is.

Conversation skills

Once the conversation is going, there are several other cues of interest. These cues are good indicators that a woman is interested in continuing the conversation and may be interested in a man romantically. Without a doubt, the most powerful and clear signal a woman can send is touching a guy. Studies tell us that this happens less often than you might think. Instead, the guy usually does the touching, lightly touching a woman's arm or hips, or putting his hand on the small of her back or waist as she walks in front of him. Another example would be holding her hand as he leads her through the bar. All these signs are pretty clear indicators of attraction from guys, but women reciprocating those touches—because they are less likely to happen—are even more important signs.

Instead of touching the guy, women touch other things. Women will touch their hair, adjust their clothing, play with or stroke objects—like her glass or the table. All this self-touch works to draw a man in closer. He'll start considering how he might like to be touched by her hands, too. While women tend to do this more often, sometimes guys will touch their own face, especially to stroke their chin or five o'clock shadow. All these self-touches are pretty clear signs of romantic attraction—more than just being friendly.

Finally, in conversation, there are a couple of other key nonverbal signs. But all of these may come with some negative consequences. For example, a woman could pretend to pout. She could stick her lower lip out and pretend that her feelings were hurt or she is mock-sad. For some guys, especially Traditional and Physical types, this is a major turn-on. However, other guys might find it sort of silly and some women might prefer not to act this way just to get a guy interested.

A guy could lean over a woman or lean into her. This move works particularly well if a guy is bigger and taller than the woman. Essentially, he is creating a little cage around her not only to show other guys that this woman is his, but also to show off his size compared to her. As a downside, guys who lean in like this are often perceived to be more phony and arrogant, but they also succeed in seeming manly, too. Women might find a guy who does this overaggressive, which would be a major turnoff for Polite and non-Traditional women. By comparison, a Traditional woman will find it very attractive because she likes guys who know how to take charge.

FREQUENT, EASY TO SEE, BUT INCONSISTENTLY RELATED TO ATTRACTION

The last group of signs of attraction are those that people do all the time, but tend to be just as much signs of attraction as evidence of being outgoing, friendly or having a good time.

Smile

Make no mistake; this one comes up a lot! It is a sure-fire sign of engagement and interest for both men and women. Smiles are a way of saying, "I'm enjoying this interaction." People who smile more are more successful at speed dating. People like other people who smile and will smile back at them. Although there are several studies that say that a lot of smiling is associated with greater romantic interest and sexual availability, it is not absolutely clear that this is a sign of romantic interest rather than enjoyment or friendship. You must remember this; sometimes a smile is just a smile.

Talk with your hands

People who are more engaged also talk with their hands more, and consequently experience more speed-dating success. When a woman talks with her hands, it is a pretty good indicator that she is interested in keeping the conversation going. Expressiveness is a very attractive quality in creating good rapport and in dating. But, again, people also talk with their hands because they are extroverted and outgoing as well as being romantically interested.

Laughter

Everybody loves people with a sense of humor. It comes up as a top-rated quality over and over again. During a first conversation, men and women will try to get each other laughing. Although a guy is typically making the jokes, he also does more of the laughing. He laughs to let a woman know that what he is saying is meant to be funny, and he laughs at things that have no resemblance to humor just to show that he is fun-loving and joyful. But, more than anything, guys laugh because they are interested in the woman they are chatting with. And if a guy can get a woman to laugh, he will take it as a very good sign that the conversation is going well. In fact, very savvy and socially aware women will actually fake-laugh for a guy's benefit (like Liz Lemon's Julia Roberts laugh).

All of this is well and good, but the majority of people who go out with their friends are looking to have fun, and laughter is a key part of that. Laughing is contagious and a great way to bond with people. People laugh for all kinds of reasons and because they have all kinds of dispositions—not just because they are flirting. This is certainly a sign of engagement, but it is not a definitive sign of romantic interest.

Mutual eye contact

Straying eyes are a bad sign. The more time that people spend looking directly at one another, the more interested they are, especially men. However, making eye contact is something that people generally do if they are trying to be socially appropriate and be good listeners.

Clothing

Conventional wisdom would say that if men and women are dressed up, then they are dressed to impress the opposite sex. In particular, if women are dressed in a sexy or bold fashion, one would assume that they are trying to get men's attention. Indeed, if a woman is dressed in a more seductive manner, her romantic intentions can be read more easily. However, this isn't so straightforward. The X factor is whether she is already in a relationship. A lot of women who go out with their boyfriends dress in the sexiest and boldest outfits they can find (lucky guys!). As a consequence, if you are at a club and see a sexily clad lady, her attire alone won't let you know if she is taken or not. But if she *is* single, then her choice of attire indicates that she is typically open to meeting new men and flirting.

RESEARCH SAYS

Men can more accurately distinguish sexually interested women from those who are not interested when the women are provocatively dressed.

Yes, body language can give you some important information about whether a person is flirting or not. But, body language is incredibly ambiguous. In fact, people are often intentionally ambiguous to protect themselves from social disapproval and rejection. Most people's nonverbal behavior will indicate that they are putting themselves out there just a little bit, but not too far. We can rarely know for sure that people are interested unless they walk up and say, "I'm interested in you." And this leads us to Rule #5...

RULE #5 The fear of rejection or looking bad makes flirting less direct.

Fear of Rejection

The other problem of knowing when someone is flirting is that people are usually incredibly inconsistent for one simple reason—they hate being rejected. People want to seem friendly, but not too friendly because being an overly eager person is a turnoff. They want to look good, but not overly vain because vanity is a turnoff. They want to appear interested, but not too interested because apparently everyone in the singles scene can smell desperation. This "not too much" rule is due to the sad reality of rejection. There is always the lingering threat of being turned down or finding out someone is already taken no matter how well a conversation is going. People almost never come right out and say, "I am interested in you and we should get to know each other to see if we will sleep together tonight."

Even though this information is readily available in a personal ad, in real life people don't walk around with signs on their necks indicating whether they are available. When asking a classmate out or during a blind date, you never know what you are getting into. So people are inconsistent in their nonverbal actions because they want to be able to maintain plausible deniability if they're rejected.

Trying Too Hard

Trying to look good may have the unintended consequence of looking fake, phony or trying too hard. A flirt who is too obvious or exaggerated in displaying interest may come off poorly. A man who winks and flexes his muscles too obviously becomes a joke, not a successful flirt. A woman who touches a man early and frequently may be perceived as trying too hard (especially by other women), even though some men (like Physical flirts) may appreciate the clear signal of interest. Laughing too hard or too loudly, smiling too much or just being too obvious is counterproductive. You can't fix the problem of being obvious by overdoing it. You must always strike a balance.

RULE #6 Flirting is *not* just about sexual or romantic attraction.

Now that we've looked at all the signs that someone is probably interested and not just being friendly, we get to the more murky land of figuring out whether you are a pawn in someone else's game. As you now know, different flirting styles are related to different relationship goals. The best example of this is the Playful style, where flirting is more or less disconnected from romantic interest. Beyond the Playful style, there are a lot of reasons people flirt. A flirt may be trying to make a third party jealous, might be a little drunk and uninhibited, or may just be seeking attention.

Because some people are able to act in a way they don't feel, it is very difficult to know whether any group of verbal or nonverbal signs are linked to a specific goal of initiating a relationship, much less a long-term relationship. Consider this: If people are acting very straightforward, showing all the obvious signs of attraction, then we are often suspicious of their motives. We doubt their interest in us. It makes sense that this is the situation Playful flirts often finds themselves in. Their friends or anyone else who has experience talking with them doubt whether they are interested in anything serious.

What to do about it?

Short of asking them directly, "Where is this going?" there aren't a lot of alternatives. My best suggestion for you is to figure out their flirting style and then work backward to their goals. By knowing what their flirting style looks like and talks like, you can use that to guess what they really want to happen. In Chapter 9, "Common Mistakes and Helpful Hints," I go into more detail about how to detect another person's flirting style.

RULE #7 Women are in control of the interaction.

THE SURVEY SAYS

When women flirt, nearly 80 percent of men flirt back. When men flirt, only 60 percent of women flirt back.

This is something that both men and women know in their hearts, but need to face up to in reality. The little statistic in the box from the eHarmony Survey tells us an important story. Women are better able to get men's attention than men are able to get women's attention. This also echoes what researchers have been saying for years. Women start most interactions by showing they are interested in being approached, through signals like eye contact and quick glances. Then, during the conversation, women strongly influence how men act. How dynamic and charming a man is depends on how responsive, friendly and fun women are. True, some men are more confident, charming and attractive, but women play a big role in confirming whether or not men's charm is welcome. Women determine how men behave when flirting, more than men determine how women behave.

QUOTABLE

"Flirting is the gentle art of making a man feel pleased with himself."

—Helen Rowland, American author and humorist

Here are some examples. Some guys are convinced they are hot stuff, and they may strut around bars as if they own the place. These guys may pick up women, but they also get shot down a whole lot, too. If you think about it, it isn't the guys who are making this happen. It is whether or not a woman agrees with the man's perception of himself. Let's say a woman wants to get something out of a guy. A Playful flirt told me a great story about how she convinced this police officer to let her out of a ticket.

She acted so sorry and oh so helpless, and the officer ate it up. Was he a Derek Morgan from TV's *Criminal Minds* or a Barney Fife? It doesn't matter. She made it happen. Not him.

Consider the fact that some of the best studies of nonverbal flirting have shown that the most influence a guy has is influencing a woman to continue to pay attention to him. His actions do matter, but only if she likes what she sees. From that point on, she makes it easy or hard on him to continue. Amazingly, this often leads him to believe that he himself has initiated the approach and is successfully making the conversation move forward. He isn't consciously processing the come-on from her.

Women, if you want a man to act his best during your first interaction, let him know nonverbally that he is doing a good job. Men, your best bet is to trust your gut. If the conversation is going well, then she probably wants it to continue. If it is going poorly, then bail out. It is unlikely to get better by your actions, attraction or moves.

RULE #8 You can be clearer.

Basically, there are two ways that you can be clearer in getting your message across: by saying so and by acting like it. Saying so doesn't have to require a stark admission of attraction, and acting like it doesn't have to come off as desperate. In both cases, your best way to be clear is to be consistent.

Saying So

OK, I've been saying over and over that nobody comes out and admits to being interested, but there are certainly things you can do to clarify your point. Remember in Chapter 7, "The Switch," where I told you about the idea of a relational frame? You have got to frame your interaction in terms of flirting and dating, not just friendliness or having a good conversation. In other words, you need to be more explicit. A direct message can convey romantic feelings and clarify that you want to be more than friends. How? You have got to be both planned and natural by planning out a few words to say and letting your body language follow its natural course.

GUYS

For guys, there are three messages you can deliver to clarify your romantic intentions. The first is compliments. Compliments are one of the very few messages that reframe a message as romantic as opposed to friendly. People like to be praised, even when they know the other person is doing it to curry favor. But don't be too sexually aggressive or cheesy. Be attentive and sincere in your compliments. Try to pay attention to something that looked like it took effort or might inspire a good story, like a necklace or a tattoo.

The second suggestion in conversation is figuring out her relationship status. Women don't really like it when men come out and say, "Are you single?" But that question is remarkably effective at letting her know you're interested. If a man can establish that she is available, then it is a good way of letting her know that he is interested in something more.

The last conversational strategy is also pretty obvious: arrange to see her again. As long as a guy doesn't act like an ass or isn't terribly unattractive, he usually will be able to get a girl's number between 40 percent and 60 percent of the time. For the Sincere and Polite flirts out there, this is also a great way to move the relationship out of the friend zone immediately. "It was really nice meeting you" just doesn't cut it. You have to establish romantic interest early on, if you are a Polite or Sincere flirt, and asking for her digits is one way to do it.

LADIES

There are several ways women can show interest. The first is to laugh and laugh often. This is a great way to keep the conversation going and a great way to show a guy you are interested in what he has to say. Laughing conveys enough warmth and interest to keep a guy talking, but not too much risk if you were to put yourself out there.

Second, if you are so bold, try a very simple pickup line. A classic study on pickup lines found out that when women used a simple pickup line they were successful between 80 percent and 100 percent of the time (which are much better odds than guys got). If they said something sweet, like "I feel embarrassed about this, but I'd like to get to know you," it was incredibly successful. Drinks, attention and requests for phone numbers followed nearly every single time. Don't bother with cheesy or silly lines. Instead, lines that are sweet and friendly are very well-received by guys: "I saw you and thought, 'I'm going to kick myself all night if I don't at least come over and say Hi.'" or "I'm sort of shy, but I'd like to find out more about you."

Third, try to get a guy you like to ask for your number. One way to think about this is to try to clarify your mutual interests by finding out if there is any reason he might need your help in the future: "If you ever want to find out more about that biking trail I was telling you about, you should look me up." Women are very successful when they get men to ask for their number because it makes guys feel in control, but gives her a way to be more forward without having to wait around for him. Besides, guys love it, too.

> ### RESEARCH SAYS
>
> When chatting up somebody, you've got about 10 minutes to make an impression. And the last few minutes count the most.

Acting Like It

To get started on the body language part of this, it is important to know what *channel consistency* is. Each of the various ways we communicate using our bodies is called a channel. For example, our eyes are one channel and our arms are another. *Channel consistency* means that all the channels are sending the same message. Channel inconsistency is another way of saying, "You are sending mixed messages." Being too subtle in displaying romantic interest or being channel-inconsistent makes it hard for others to know what you think of them. For example, you may be smiling and nodding, but you may also be closing off your body by crossing your arms, leaning away or showing uneasiness.

The two clearest negative signals a woman shows in her body language are crossing her legs and moving her legs away from a guy when talking to him. Doing this seems to indicate that she is already on her way out of the door. By being an inconsistent flirter, you make it hard for another person to get your message. To be clear, you can show your interest repeatedly through several different channels at the same time. The bottom line: Inconsistent body language makes for confusing flirting.

RULE #9 You can be more accurate.

Watch

If you want to know whether someone is flirting with you, the first thing you have to do is start watching. You need to pay better attention to what people are doing with their bodies, their voices and their eyes, and whether they are sending signs of interest. This is true even before the conversation starts. The most successful guy out there isn't the one who approaches the most women, but the one who approaches women who are watching him. Once in a conversation, watch for the most obvious signs of attraction, but don't expect them. You are better off trying to get a general impression than keeping a running tally of nonverbal signs. If you feel the conversation isn't going anywhere, trust your instinct and bow out early. If it *is* going well, then you should say or do something to switch relational frames to indicate your own interest.

Finally, it helps to have an outside point of view. People who are already in a romantic relationship are better able to guess the romantic interests of others. Although it would be ideal if your friends who are currently in relationships would introduce you to people they know, it would also help if they were at the bar or club and watched you interact. Chances are they have a more accurate perspective than you do about your own behavior.

Listen

Listen for signs that the other person is interested, like questions about your own relationship status and self-promoting statements. By far, the most common way that people try to get others to like them is to talk about the things they are good at. They will brag, but not too obviously. If someone is talking about the things that matter to them and making sure you know they are a good catch, even by being modest, it is a good way to determine that they are flirting.

Learn

Look, I'm going to be blunt. You are going to have to learn to get comfortable talking to strangers. This is going to take practice. However, it doesn't have to be just at a bar or club. Although people there are more open to meeting strangers, people get to know one another at all kinds of places, like gyms, libraries, museums, grocery stores and coffee shops. In all those places, there is a possibility of meeting someone. This means you have to start watching more closely and becoming more open to meeting someone by surprise.

Chapter Nine

COMMON MISTAKES AND HELPFUL HINTS

At this point you are probably asking yourself, *This is a lot of information about flirting styles, switches and flirtatious cues. What I really want to know is how I can use that information to get the results I'm looking for. How am I going to win over my crush?* Welcome to Chapter 9, which is dedicated to showing you how to make your flirting style work for you. Here you'll find out where each flirting style typically goes wrong and what you can do to improve your chances.

This chapter is laid out like a night on the town or hanging out with friends. We'll start at your home turf. Where you look for love is one of the most important decisions you'll make. After considering your best route to romance, I'll tell you what sort of people will find your flirting style most appealing. Research shows that you benefit the most when your flirting style matches up with the flirting style of your crush. Then, I'll give you some conversation pointers and helpful hints, including how to detect another person's flirting style, how to proceed if things are going well and how to bow out gracefully if they aren't. By the end of this chapter, you'll have all the information you need to communicate your own interest clearly and determine whether or not your crush is attracted to you, too.

RETURN TO HOME TURF

In Chapter 1, "The Five Flirting Styles," I explained the three pathways to romance: the Hookup, the First Date and the Known Quantity. Throughout this book, I wanted to impress upon you that there is more than one way to start a relationship. To build on this idea, rather than seeking love in a place totally unsuited to your style of flirting, you can look for love in the place you have the best chance of meeting someone who shares and prefers your style of flirting—like having a home field advantage. If you prefer relaxed conversation to dancing at a crowded club, maybe a dinner party or even a coffee shop in the afternoon would be a better venue for you to flirt. Do yourself a favor and seek out love wherever you feel most comfortable—the place that best suits your flirting style.

If You Prefer the Hookup

HOW DOES THIS WORK?

The hookup pathway thrives at bars, clubs and parties. You know the environment is set for a hookup when the place is hyper-social, the music is pumping, people are dressed to impress and alcohol is abundant.

WHAT STYLES DO IT WELL?

The Physical and the Playful flirting styles do this best. They are very comfortable directly communicating their romantic interest and using strategies that work at bars and parties, like playing games or teasing. From time to time, Traditional flirts go the hookup route, especially if they're at a club or in a classy atmosphere. The Traditional flirt's pathway to romance can either be a fairy-tale (white knight and princess) romance or the slow-go approach. If you start at the club and are a Traditional flirt, then you are probably looking for a fairy-tale romance, especially if you are a Traditional man.

COMMON CHALLENGES

Unless you are a Playful or Physical guy, it might be extremely painful to get up the nerve to approach women at a bar or club. The same goes for women. Men in this atmosphere are too assertive or forward for your tastes. One thing to keep in mind is that if your flirting style doesn't match this environment, it might be best just to avoid it. If you find yourself in such a place, don't bother trying to pick up someone—it isn't your scene. You can do better elsewhere.

ADJUST YOUR SWITCH

In this atmosphere, you need to flip your switch on, if it isn't on already. Remember this: when men approach women at a bar, the guy is flirting—plain and simple. You need to adjust your internal compass to start picking up on it, accepting that interest, and—if you are interested, too—reciprocating it. Playing nice with others gets you bonus points.

RELATIONSHIP EXPECTATIONS

One final thing about starting romance on the hookup path—it probably is unlikely to end in a long-term relationship. Hookups at a bar only end up leading to a serious relationship about 12 percent of the time, and very few respondents to the FSI Survey met their last partner at a bar or club. The other 88 percent of the time, these relationships are just a one-night thing, not a long-term thing. If this is what you want and your flirting style fits the bill, then happy hunting!

If You Prefer the Known Quantity

HOW DOES THIS WORK?

The known quantity pathway happens any time that you are romantically interested in someone you already know. This includes potential partners from school, work or someone in your group of friends. Because it is someone you already know, you are well past the get-to-know-you conversations. You have a different challenge—how to take it to the next level.

WHAT STYLES DO IT WELL?

Polite flirts are very comfortable in this domain, particularly if they are approaching someone they met at their place of worship. This complements their respectful and rule-governed way of doing things. Traditional flirts are also on this pathway if they are on the slow-go approach to romance (think *Pride and Prejudice*). Sincere flirts are also quite familiar with this route because they are usually stuck in the friend zone, trying to convert a close friendship into something more intimate.

COMMON CHALLENGES

Unlike the bar or club scene, the challenge here isn't approaching your crush or picking out a person with potential. You have already done that. (Kudos! Picking someone with potential isn't easy.) The known quantity route requires a different set of strategies. Just because some move works in a bar does not mean it will go over well in everyday life. Remember Noah from the Polite chapter, who tried to use a pickup line on a friend he was interested in? She wanted nothing to do with it. The challenge of the known quantity is making your crush notice that you want something more than a friendship. (I include strategies for determining if your friend shares your interest and what to do about it in a bonus chapter, called "The Friend Zone" that can be found on my website at www.FlirtingStyles.com.)

ADJUST YOUR SWITCH

If you are already on this path, you probably haven't made your move yet. Maybe you weren't even sure you were interested until now. I'm guessing that your switch is off most of the time. This isn't necessarily a bad thing—it is probably what allowed you to get to know your potential crush in a safe and nonthreatening way to begin with. But, now you need to get switched on to start communicating your attraction more clearly, and you need to start looking for and accepting cues that she is interested in you, too. This will help your crush get the message that you are interested in romance, not just friendship. Check out suggestions for how to get switched on in Chapter 7, "The Switch."

If You Prefer the First Date

HOW DOES THIS WORK?

The first date route can take many forms—maybe you finally got up the nerve to ask out an attractive coworker, met someone online and are meeting face-to-face for the first time, or met someone at a bar and then asked her out on a date. However you got here, you are now going to meet face-to-face and sit down to talk for a while on a real, live date.

WHAT STYLES DO IT WELL?

As I mentioned in Chapter 5, the Sincere style loves the first date. The whole purpose of a first date is to do things a Sincere flirt does well—talk, get to know each other, share and learn. If you first met your date through the internet, you also might feel less apprehensive getting to know him better face-to-face because you have already had a more formal online conversation with extra time to peruse his profile for clues to his personality and preferences. The first date is a very good place to be for the Polite or Traditional flirt.

COMMON CHALLENGES

Later in this chapter I offer seven helpful hints for having a good conversation with someone you are interested in romantically. All these apply to the first date pathway. One of the advantages of the first date route is that it is pretty clear why you are there: you both are interested in learning more about the potential of a romantic relationship and whether or not each feels some sexual chemistry, too. Getting to the first date stage is exceptionally valuable for Sincere and Polite flirts, whose crushes may not always realize that they're interested in anything more than friendship. For Physical and Playful styles, the challenges are different. Physical and Playful flirts have to slow things down and meet their crush halfway. They've got to adjust their switch down a notch or two so as not to come on too strong.

ADJUST YOUR SWITCH

For the Playful style, particularly, if you are on a date, it may be tough to focus on and flirt with your date, letting go of the possibility that there might be exciting potential elsewhere. This is especially important when it comes to keeping your attention on your date, not on anybody else who happens to be around—waiters and hostesses included. It also might be necessary to tone down any of the flirting strategies that are so useful at a bar, like being a bit dismissive, coy, playing games or being overly sarcastic. You don't have to flip your switch on for a date. You need to adjust your switch to keep your attentions focused on your date.

UNCOMMON BUT GOOD PLACES TO MEET SOMEONE

There are many possible places to meet someone that are off the radar. Here are a few for you to consider:

- **Ask your friends.** One of the best ways to approach someone is to be introduced by a mutual friend. I'm not recommending blind dates, per se, but an introduction through a friend helps to get the conversation started. It also offers you a source of follow-up information, if you want to get your date's number or find out more about him. Traditional flirts (because they have few cross-sex friends) and Playful flirts (because they don't use friendship as a path to romance) might not benefit from this approach, but this will be a great way to go for the Polite, Sincere and Physical styles.
- **Classroom.** Students can tap into the potential of meeting people in their classes. This can work for any flirting style. Try talking to prospective dates before or after class and seeing if they'd like to study with you for the next exam. This is a great way to switch contexts and get to know each other better.

- **Coffee shops.** These are somewhat intimate places where people can get to know each other quite well. There is not a lot of distraction, so be prepared to have something to say and know how to make your exit if your date is involved or not interested. A lot of coffee shops have large tables where people can work and read. Try to sit near someone who is cute and strike up a conversation if she notices (and doesn't seem to mind) your being there. Try to be direct and friendly by introducing yourself and trying to get to know her. If you have a favorite place to go, check out if anyone else goes there often; she just might be there because of you! This is a great place for the Polite or Sincere flirting styles because the atmosphere fits their flirting style and there's potential depth to the conversation.

BE NATURAL AND DO WHAT YOU DO WELL

The one thing I really want to stress about flirting and dating is for you to be comfortable doing what you already do well. If you aren't good at certain things, focus on the things and places where you are at your best. It is a lot harder to change your flirting style than to use the one you have to your advantage. Take my advice as it works for you. For example, if you are a female Traditional flirt, you believe that men should approach women first. Let's face it: you aren't going to be the one to make the first approach, so you will want to pass on my advice to use pickup lines or be more direct. Part of my reason for writing this book is to help you better understand your natural flirting style so that you can feel more comfortable with it and flirt effortlessly, rather than consciously. This will come off as much more genuine and be more effective overall.

RESEARCH SAYS

For some people, attraction just *clicks*. It is rapid and intense. There is no use trying to make it happen; just accept it if it does.

WHOM TO APPROACH

This only applies to situations where you have never met your new love interest before, not when you know the person, as in the known quantity path. But if you are trying to pick up a stranger in a bar, you need to know whom to flirt with (and whom not to).

For Men

The best suggestion for men is to be receptive to women's non-verbal cues before you try to start up a conversation. One of the best signs that a woman wants to be approached is that she will initiate eye contact at least once and likely more than once.

Keep your eyes open and approach when you are invited! Look outward to show that you are also open to a new conversation.

For Women

Guys who sit with an open posture—arms spread out in the booth—scanning the room and barely looking at the friends they came with are the ones most open to talking to someone new at a bar. To get a certain guy to approach you, the above advice applies—eye contact is a great way to get things started. Failing that, walking within his visual gaze or moving into his territory so that he accidentally bumps into you are good strategies, too.

WHY SIMILARITY IN STYLE MATTERS

Whether you are a man or a woman, you are probably wondering, *Who is going to find my flirting style appealing?* When it comes to flirting styles, do opposites attract or do birds of a feather flock together? It turns out that similarity matters most. We want a partner who communicates attraction the same way we do. No particular flirting style is most attractive or best for everyone: it is the match that counts.

What style do you want?

In the FSI Survey, I asked daters what style of communication they found attractive when first meeting someone and what types of flirting strategies they preferred. Their answers allowed me to determine whether a person's own flirting style matched their flirting preferences. Here's what I found out.

I WANT A PARTNER WITH A PHYSICAL FLIRTING STYLE IF...

I am a Physical or a Sincere flirt. If you are a Physical flirt, you are particularly attractive to other Physical flirts. However, Sincere flirts also tend to find you appealing, probably because they are open to more complementary partners and seek out physical chemistry when flirting. On the other hand, Polite and Traditional flirts aren't interested in Physical flirts. They find a Physical style a bit too aggressive. Additionally, the Physical style is most attractive to people who are open to having sex outside the confines of a long-term relationship. This is consistent with the idea that a direct style of communicating attraction clearly communicates openness to physical intimacy. (It also reinforces the whole sex on the brain thing from Chapter 2, "The Physical Style.")

I WANT A PARTNER WITH A POLITE FLIRTING STYLE IF...

I am a Polite or a Traditional flirt. This may be pretty obvious, but it is really important to say: being a Polite flirt is very appealing and attractive to people who share your style of flirting. Sometimes people with a Polite style might doubt that their way of communicating attraction is desirable. When you share a style with someone, you feel more attracted to him. Finally, whatever your own particular flirting style, women prefer men who are hands-off and well-mannered, or polite. Not only is there nothing wrong with a less assertive style, it can make all the difference in building romance with a Polite woman. This is also a good thing because Polite flirts, even if they take a lot of time to get there, really value long-term and stable romantic relationships.

I WANT A PARTNER WITH A PLAYFUL FLIRTING STYLE IF . . .

I am a Playful flirt, too. Playful flirts are truly birds of a feather in matters of love—they enjoy teasing, joking, competing and playing games with each other. On the other hand, if you are a Polite flirt, you don't want a Playful partner. Listen up, Playful style! Your way of doing things might be a turnoff for more conventional and rule-governed partners, so they probably aren't your best choice. Interestingly, Physical flirts don't find Playful flirts particularly appealing, either. Physical flirts want to experience that heady and exciting feeling of falling for someone. They don't want to be confused by someone who is flirting just for fun. Playful flirts are enjoying the boost of self-esteem, but Physical flirts are on a romantic mission. Finally, no matter what their flirting style, men love Playful women. They find the Playful style of communicating romance sexy and exciting.

I WANT A PARTNER WITH A SINCERE FLIRTING STYLE IF . . .

I am a Sincere flirt, but not a Physical or Polite flirt. A Sincere flirt is likely to forge a deep emotional connection with other Sincere flirts. However, I was surprised to find out that Sincere flirts are not particularly attractive to people who communicate attraction directly and assertively or just the opposite—in a cautious and mannered way. Why? Physical flirts may find the talking and deep conversation unappealing and a little confusing—is she really interested in me or is she trying to be friends? They might also find this type of conversation inappropriate or boring. Polite flirts may feel that a strong emotional connection is premature or too revealing. Finally, there is one more group of people who find the Sincere style more attractive: women. Men, take heed!

I WANT A PARTNER WITH A TRADITIONAL FLIRTING STYLE IF...

I am a Polite flirt. Polite flirts are very comfortable with more old-fashioned approaches to romance. By comparison, Playful flirts don't dig Traditional flirts. In addition, women really like Traditional men—much more than men like Traditional women. Men who do want a more Traditional woman have personalities that are conservative and cautious, just like their flirting style. Simply put, a Traditional worldview matches up with Traditional courtship.

WHAT STYLE IS BEST FOR ME?

IF YOU ARE A...	YOU WILL APPEAL TO...
Physical flirt	Physical flirts. Sincere flirts.
Polite flirt	Polite flirts. Traditional flirts. Women.
Playful flirt	Playful flirts. Men.
Sincere flirt	Sincere flirts. Women.
Traditional flirt	Polite flirts. Women.

REJECTION IS THE ONLY WAY TO GET RESULTS

Unfortunately, even if we have read the signals carefully and chosen our approach wisely, we all get rejected at some point. *You must keep trying.* In fact, just getting accustomed to walking up to and talking to a member of the opposite sex is a step in the right direction, especially if you are a Polite or Traditional flirt. It is important not to be afraid to put yourself out there. Being open and direct shows that you like someone enough to be willing to be rejected, and people generally find this very flattering. Whatever your style, you are going to have to take some risks to find love. While I cannot guarantee that you will find the person you're looking for by taking risks, I can guarantee that you won't find anyone if you take no risks whatsoever.

RESEARCH SAYS

Becoming more comfortable with flirting takes some trial and error. You can get better at asking someone out; a little practice goes a long way.

HOW TO HAVE A GOOD CONVERSATION

Let's say you started the conversation. Now what? Here are seven goals to guide your conversation. Each one describes the goal of the conversation. Some of these goals are about how you present yourself and others are about how you want to make your new crush feel. To get started, let me give you a metaphor about flirting through conversation.

Badminton Lobs Back and Forth: Reciprocity

When I was a kid, sometimes my brothers and I would play badminton in the summertime. Each time you smacked the birdie, it floated swiftly into the air and slowly came back down again. As long as it wasn't an overhead slam, the game kept going by lobbing the birdie up, watching it fall and then watching the other person lobbing it up again.

When you are flirting with someone, the conversation is like badminton. Your goal is to keep the conversation going by lobbing up comments, compliments, stories and questions. If your conversation partner is interested, she will hit it back your way. If the conversation drops to the floor, you've got to pick it up again. If you slam your partner with something—either a move that is too forward, a compliment that is too sexual or attention that is too straightforward—you drive the conversation into the ground. Sometimes a little quick shot, like a joke or a compliment, can be met with a quick, playful return. Either way, being lobbed to and then back again is the excitement of flirting. Like badminton, you must reciprocate flirting, each time only slightly intensifying the volley.

I was at a bar recently watching people interact (one of my favorite pastimes). I watched a guy approach a woman at the bar and buy her a drink. Throughout the night, they slowly drifted closer together, each coming nearer inch by inch, but always waiting until a move was reciprocated. Then they touched for the first time. He touched her arm near her hand. A minute later, she touched his shoulder. When she got up, she brushed up against him. Neither said, "Excuse me," or backed away. They had another drink and within the hour, they were in each other's personal space. Each move was part of a graceful game. Each signaled to the other that they were quite comfortable playing and wanted it to continue. Show interest, talk and laugh, make minor contact and so on—enjoy the game as it progresses, but don't rush the conclusion. Don't take too many turns without a returned comment or question. If the conversation lags, start a new one. If your partner doesn't want to play, let her go. There are other players to strike up a game with.

Seven Goals for Conversation

Here is some advice to play so you *both* win.

1. **Flirting is about making a connection, but that connection can come in many forms.** Physical flirts feel immediate physical chemistry, while Sincere flirts look for an emotional connection. Polite flirts privilege showing respect and kindness, and Playful flirts connect through teasing or sarcastic banter. Flirting is about making a connection. When your flirting styles match, trust that whatever connection you want to make, your partner wants to make, too. Our biggest

fear when flirting is that the other person won't find us attractive, but being attractive is only one part of it. Flirting is about connecting in a way that means something to you. If you are a Polite or Sincere flirt, think of your crush as someone who could be your friend. It's much easier for you to make a friend than it is to make someone fall in love with you. Besides, chemistry is likely to come later anyway.

2. **Talk for the next time.** Your goal is to have an enjoyable conversation with the possibility of romantic potential if you meet again. Whether in a bar, at the office, in a classroom or with a platonic friend you secretly like, be someone your partner would like to talk to again. No matter how long or short the conversation and no matter where it takes place, you should talk with the understanding that you will have another chance with her. By keeping focused on this next time, you will not be under the illusion that this is your one and only chance. Being too worried about making it perfect the first time is only likely to rush things unnecessarily or create anxiety. Assume that there will be a next time, because that is what it means to be successful.

3. **Be genuinely interested.** If you take genuine interest in someone, he can sense it. Spending too much time talking about yourself or not paying attention to what he is saying will spoil your chance of getting to know him. Each of us wants to feel that we are interesting. Convey that interest by treating him as if he were the

only one in the room—no matter who you are or where that room may be.

4. **Get her talking.** If a guy can ask good questions and get a woman talking, it shows that he is interested, that he is a good listener and that he wants to learn more about her. Do not be so self-focused as to be perceived as uninterested. Ruling the conversation is rarely an effective way of communicating that you are interested in anyone except yourself. In fact, a guy talking too much is a good indication that the woman he is talking to *isn't* interested! This goal applies to women, too. Do not forget that guys are also flattered when they are asked to talk about themselves.

5. **Make him feel wanted.** When flirting, it is a good idea to make your crush feel attractive and desirable. However, this has an added benefit: it makes your crush want you in return. Feeling that someone is interested in you is a turn-on. For some flirting styles, this is a difficult thing to do. If your switch is generally off, this is going to require flipping your switch on. A little dose of sexuality in your interaction, even if it is only in your head, will help to communicate your attraction and help get that feeling coming back your way. And if your switch is on, you'll be able to pick up on his attraction, too!

6. **Laugh.** Laughter is a great way to build chemistry. Displaying a good sense of humor is "the single most effective tactic men use to attract women." There are many reasons laughter works: it makes people

feel united and on the same team. Laughing says you
share similar ideas about what is funny, and you share
values and beliefs, too. It shows empathy and the
ability to take another person's perspective. Being able
to make and get jokes may be a sign of intelligence,
too. This goal should be very comfortable for most
flirting styles, particularly Playful and Sincere flirts.
However, Polite flirts may need to let their guard down
a little and laugh—I promise it will make everyone feel
more relaxed.

7. **At some point, frame your conversation as flirting.**
    This advice is for those who are pursuing the known
    quantity route, especially those who are friends first.
    Friendship requires treating someone you like as
    an equal or as someone you respect. When flirting,
    many people (women especially) are unaccustomed
    to being treated this way by men who are interested.
    At some point, you must frame the interaction as
    flirting. Draw her attention to your attraction through
    compliments, questions and requests for future
    contact. Compliments, especially about dress or
    appearance, can be a bit forward for certain flirting
    styles, like Polite and Traditional, but are clear ways to
    show interest in something more. Asking whether she
    is involved is another way. This is widely interpreted
    as indicative of wanting something besides friendship.
    Finally, even if the interaction is brief, ask for her
    contact information, so you can see her again (or, at
    least, be able to make her your Facebook friend). This

helps to show that you are looking to get to know her better, and it is also a subtle type of compliment.

For Traditional Women, "Flirt to Convert"

Because none of these conversational goals is obviously flirting, hopefully many Polite and Traditional flirts can feel a lot more comfortable about what it means to flirt. Using these goals, a Traditional woman might find it easier to keep a conversation going with a guy. If you get a clear sign that he is into you, then flirt by hinting around, essentially encouraging him to keep approaching. If the man does not respond to a woman's hints and flirtation, then he may be a Polite or Traditional flirt. This doesn't mean that he isn't interested; it just means that a chivalrous and fast-paced romance isn't happening—you are on the slower route. You've got to keep trying to convert his relational frame toward romance by reminding him that there is something else going on. For particularly Traditional guys, this may take some time. These men need some extra attention to convey that you are open to his attentions.

SINCERE FLIRTS, DON'T GET TOO DEEP; PLAYFUL FLIRTS, SHOW SOME DEPTH

Sincere flirts need to be aware that there is a time and place for a deep conversation—and the bar isn't it. Take a cue from Playful flirts and remember that having fun, laughing and joking, and keeping it light may be the best things to do when you first meet someone. Save the conversation for your first date. Playful flirts run into the opposite problem. This constant levity and focus on trying to get something out of flirting conveys the message that the Playful flirt has little interest in romance. If you are talking with someone you believe has relationship potential, you have to take a cue from the Sincere flirt and be more honest and personal at some point.

When it comes to flirting, we want to be able to be honest and true to ourselves, but we also want to be liked. However, we aren't always honest because we are afraid of being rejected, and without being honest, we may not be liked for who we really are. If you think of flirting as a slow escalation of attention, attraction, disclosure and contact, then it isn't an all-or-nothing thing. Instead, serve up attention that is honest and true to your flirting style and look for a return. If you like what you see in another person, always reciprocate; don't make your crush do all the work! Rather than trying to have your cake and eat it, too, share your cake, one little bite at a time.

Is there a better way to tell if someone is interested?

While some people are much better at judging whether someone is flirting than others and some people are more readable than others, in general people just aren't very good at accurately judging whether someone is flirting or just being nice. What can you do about this? I had several recommendations in Chapter 8, "Perceptions and Misperceptions," to improve your accuracy and deliver a clear message. Below is a quick list of what to look for by flirting style.

IS YOUR CRUSH INTERESTED?

- **A Playful flirt is flirting** when he seems to be totally into you, but then suddenly disappears.
- **A Playful flirt is *not* flirting** for romantic reasons, unless you know her well enough to tell that she is interacting with you in an uncharacteristic way.
- **A Physical flirt is flirting** when he displays sexual interest like a LED sign: buying drinks, dropping lines, showing off his body and dance moves, and escalating physically.
- **A Physical flirt is *not* flirting** when she doesn't feel physical chemistry. You only get this kind of attention from her when she is truly interested and attracted.
- **A Sincere flirt is flirting** when he wants to get to know you and connect emotionally, no matter where you meet.
- **A Sincere flirt is *not* flirting** through small talk or chitchat or through physical contact and touches. Although she

likes to be given compliments and is open to more forward flirting, she probably won't be the one initiating it.

- **A Traditional flirt is flirting** when he does everything first and she waits for his lead.
- **A Traditional flirt is *not* flirting** when a woman is in control or both are equally taking charge.
- **A Polite flirt is flirting** when he respects your boundaries, is attentive and respectful, but is utterly nonsexual.
- **A Polite flirt is *not* flirting** when she's in a relationship, when she's not romantically interested or she's not physically attracted. If a Polite flirt is flirting with you in an obvious way, she really means it.

ENDING THE CONVERSATION

There are two reasons to end your flirting attempts: it isn't going anywhere or it is going well but for some reason beyond your control the conversation has to end (for instance, her friends are leaving). Here's some advice for knowing when to end things and how to handle it.

Know When to Call It Quits

The cold, hard truth is that some people are going to be unreceptive for whatever reason and it's best to just move on. You've got to know when enough is enough.

How do you know when it's over? You have to trust your gut. In Chapter 8, "Perceptions and Misperceptions," I gave you some nonverbal behaviors to look for. I've also given you a list of clues that someone is one type of flirt or another and some clear verbal indications that someone is interested. But, at some level, you just have to get a feel for how the other person is responding to you, even if you don't know how or why you've come to that conclusion. If you conclude that he isn't interested, you need to follow that instinct and let go.

FOR GUYS, KNOW WHEN TO QUIT

Women do not like a guy who constantly pressures her to try to get her to talk, dance or drink. There is a point where you should be able to recognize when a woman is blatantly ignoring you or not responding to your attempts at conversation. Many times guys look only for negative signs and assume that if she doesn't leave or actively reject him, she is responding positively. However, this is rarely the case. Guys are overly optimistic when there are no clear signs of rejection. A lack of positive feedback should also give an equally clear message that she isn't interested.

FOR WOMEN, COMMUNICATE YOUR LACK OF INTEREST CLEARLY

When women don't like what men are saying, they are more likely to show it than say it. When she is unhappy, her body language (crossed arms, a sudden interest in anything other than what you have to say) will let you know before her words will. However, a lot of women are very concerned about looking or being nice. This will only confuse an aggressive guy. He cannot distinguish her niceness from flirting. Guys are also prone to wishful thinking; one of the most consistent research findings is that men overestimate a woman's flirtatiousness. If you aren't into him, you may have to be blunt. If you do not feel comfortable doing something with him, such as dancing, be firm verbally and nonverbally with him. If you give him mixed signals, he will only become confused.

Ending a Conversation, But Planning to Meet Again

Very few first-time interactions result in sex or love. Instead, you have got to meet again (and again and again). This means that you want to end your first interaction in a way that indicates you want to do it again.

One thing to keep in mind is that if you feel that the conversation went well, there is good reason to believe that it did. Trust your gut. If you are on your home turf, there are lots of reasons to believe that your gut is telling you the truth. If you decide not to ask for her digits, make that decision because you don't want to talk with her again, not because you're worried she doesn't feel the same way. You have to take risks and, all things considered, this is a pretty safe risk.

ASK FOR YOUR DATE'S NUMBER

If you ask for your crush's number, there is a good chance that she will give it to you. My research puts your odds around 40 percent if you are male and around 65 percent if you are female, which echoes research from speed-dating contexts. Asking for her number lets her know that you're interested in seeing her again, too. Failing to ask for her number is a good sign that you aren't interested or just want to be friends.

RESEARCH SAYS

According to speed-dating studies, women are chosen for dates by about half of men they meet while speed dating, and men are chosen for dates by one-third of women they meet during a speed-dating event.

SAY IT

If you are interested in getting to know him better, then say it. This is particularly tricky for Sincere and Polite flirts because they don't communicate romantic interest as clearly as other styles. Remember the frame from Chapter 7, "The Switch"? Conventional get-to-know-you conversations may frame the interaction as friendship instead of romance. This means it is hard to escalate a relationship beyond friendship. Being complimentary or direct in stating your interest will increase the chance that your motives will be interpreted as sexual or romantic. Simply saying, "I had a great time talking with you, and I would like to see you again sometime soon. Can I get your number?" is direct and effective, yet still Polite and Sincere.

ASK AROUND

If you know your crush's friends, they can make a huge difference in propelling a relationship to another level, especially if your mutual friend is a woman. Women like to play match-maker and are better at it than men are. Let's say you failed to get across the message that you were interested the first time around or are wondering if your crush felt the same way. By asking about your crush through friends, you can get her contact information or find out whether the attraction was mutual. This can help out tremendously. But be forewarned: the mutual friend needs to think you are a good catch for this to work. Otherwise, she might stop your progress cold.

THE SCENARIO: YOU WANT TO SEND A FLIRTY ONLINE DATING MESSAGE

The emerging world of online dating has introduced a whole new set of challenges when flirting. Online dating messages must strike a balance between playfulness and formality and that first online message is critical. Here are some dos and don'ts that apply to everyone, no matter what your flirting style.

Do spend time reviewing his profile carefully. Once you see something that catches your interest, make sure you draw attention to things the two of you honestly share or both really care about. Don't exaggerate or fake interest in something. That's a path to dating disap-pointment. A thoughtful message that refers back to his profile lets him know that you took the time to read it and are genuinely interested.

Don't use too many text-messaging conventions like emoticons and shorthand. These tend to come off very poorly when people don't have much else to go on except that single online message. A well-used ;) is good, but too much LMAO will get you no response. While you're at it, spell-check and edit carefully. Don't get written off because you look like you didn't take the time to even bother rereading what you wrote before pushing send.

Do be flirty by suggesting what the two of you might enjoy doing together someday. Show a sense of humor and a sense of fun about yourself and what you care about. Flirting in a way that makes sense to you and your own flirting style will help send the right message.

Don't spend too much time talking about yourself. Avoid too many "I" statements about how special you are and focus on what the two of you might share instead. Express your interest in her, not in yourself.

Don't reuse the same message for each person. Each message needs to be personal and real. Be careful that you don't come off as so formal or impersonal that the real you is utterly hidden. Form letters are best saved for the rejection pile, not for the acceptance one.

CONCLUSION

It is my hope that this book has been a useful journey of self-discovery for you. If the Flirting Styles Inventory and the contents of this book have helped you learn more about your own way of communicating attraction, then perhaps that self-reflection will get you closer to finding the love you really want. By sharing the collective insight of thousands, I hope you have gained the insight you need to overcome the challenges of dating and feel a renewed sense of optimism to overcome whatever setbacks you might face.

Finding someone to love and being loved by someone are the greatest rejuvenating, sustaining and enduring joys of life. I hope that what you have discovered in learning about your own flirting style brings you closer to finding love in your life.

Epilogue

SPENCER & KELSEY

Let's return to our star-crossed lovers from the Introduction. After that night of missed opportunities, Spencer got serious about figuring out why he couldn't seem to get his message across to Kelsey. Luckily, Spencer and I are friends, and I had shared the Flirting Styles Inventory with him a while ago. He found out that he was highly Polite and Traditional, moderate on Sincere, but low on Physical and Playful. He guessed that Kelsey was pretty Playful, but he couldn't tell the rest. I asked him to let me know how it went with Kelsey, and whether I might share his story. Here is my retelling of what happened to Spencer and Kelsey, because, after all, everyone loves a happy ending.

Wasting no time, Spencer decided that work was the best place to begin, since Playful styles tend to meet people at work.

He stopped by to talk to Kelsey, as he always did. She was busy and a bit distracted, but she looked up at him and smiled in the way that always seemed to knock him off his feet a little. Temporarily forgetting his plan, he started chatting with her about work, work and more work. He knew that one of his strengths was being empathetic and kind, and he knew he had to switch relationship frames and shift contexts. Talking about work wasn't going to get that done.

Breaking with his Polite style, he remembered that Playful flirts like compliments. He noticed that her lovely dark hair was put up for a change. Spencer said, "I think you did something different with your hair. It looks great! I like it."

Kelsey was having an awful morning. She was feeling a bit down about herself, especially her relationship life. When Spencer walked up, she felt uneasy. He had been cool to her since that night at the bar. In the past couple of weeks, she had tried to be her normal flirty self, but it didn't seem to make a difference. She called on herself to perk up when she saw Spencer coming—after all, he was still the nicest guy she knew and a great work friend. During the conversation, he did something unexpected; he commented on her hair. *Well, that was different,* she thought. Although surprised, she liked that he noticed. Kelsey laughed, "I didn't do anything special. I did it to get it out of my way."

OK. That didn't work, thought Spencer. Undeterred, he remembered his Traditional flirting style and tried the more direct approach—a context switch. He said, "Look, Kelsey. I know it is sort of out of the blue, but would you like to get dinner with me this weekend?"

Kelsey looked stunned, but readily agreed, "Yeah, that'd be really nice, Spence." Spencer was elated, and relieved. They had dinner plans, so at least this part of his plan had worked.

On their first date, Spencer was in his element and Kelsey felt a bit unsure of herself. She was not used to meeting guys for dates or sitting down for a long dinner. Spencer was charming, polite and did everything by the book. He opened doors, pulled out chairs, suggested food she might like and even ordered some great wine. Kelsey felt that she was being treated like a lady, and she loved it. Spencer also made a point of complimenting her dress. For Kelsey, this was totally unexpected: Was this really Spencer?

As the night went on, Kelsey felt out of place in the formal atmosphere and suggested they go to a bar for an after-dinner drink. Spencer agreed. There she was much more at home. She resisted the urge to have a little chat with the bartender when he came to take their order. Instead, she kept her attention on Spencer.

Soon after, Spencer offered to take her home. Kelsey was a little tipsy, while Spencer had limited his drinks. She was starting to get a little looser, more flirtatious, and Spencer felt a bit out of his element. She seemed attracted to him. Although he was very excited, he felt totally unprepared. He didn't really think this was going to happen so soon. When Kelsey invited him to come inside, he hesitated. He started to get more anxious and apprehensive. He really cared about Kelsey, so rather than trying anything, he leaned in to give her a hug and say goodnight.

Kelsey awkwardly accepted his hug—sort of that head dodging, weird arm placement, are-you-going-to-kiss-me thing. After that was over, she looked up into Spencer's eyes, then quickly downward. When she glanced up again, he was looking straight into her eyes. She said, "I had a really great night, Spencer."

Spencer was totally smitten. He opened his mouth to say something, but nothing came out. Bolstering his courage, he leaned down to kiss her, politely hoping she'd want the same.

And she did.

Appendix

ABOUT THE PROCEDURES IN THIS BOOK

There are many claims in this book. Whenever the claim was taken from a source other than my own research, a full citation is provided in the Endnotes. For example, claims about the ability to read whether or not a man is flirting came from peer-reviewed publications and are cited accordingly. By contrast, all claims about the flirting styles are drawn from four research projects that I designed alone or with collaborators. To my knowledge, no other published study has used the Flirting Styles Inventory.

SAMPLES

The first sample (known throughout the book as the eHarmony Survey) of 5,020 individuals came from eHarmony volunteers recruited through an electronic newsletter in February 2007. This original survey data was collected over approximately six weeks. All respondents in the final sample completed all measures on the survey and were screened for faked data. The procedures are reported in greater detail in "Individual Differences in the Communication of Romantic Interest: Development of the Flirting Styles Inventory" by Jeffrey Hall, Steve Carter, Michael Cody, and Julie Albright, and published in *Communication Quarterly* in 2010.

Participants in the second sample (known throughout the book as the FSI Survey) were recruited through a link associated with the online Flirting Styles Inventory. These data were collected from September 6, 2010 through April 6, 2011. Individuals who completed the flirting styles portion of the survey and the first two study measures (i.e., big five personality, ambivalent sexism inventory) were kept for analysis. Although not all respondents completed the entire survey, missing data was not imputed (i.e., added back in through statistical methods). Respondents were removed when the two questions about age or the two questions about gender did not match (for example, the question, "What is your age?" was more than two years different than the age calculated from the question, "In what year were you born?"). Roughly 3 percent were removed for mismatch. The final sample included 4,472 respondents. Half of the volunteers were from the United States, and at least three people were from each of the 50 states and Puerto Rico and Washington, D.C. Like the eHarmony Survey, about two-thirds were women and single, and the average age of this sample was 32.

The third sample was drawn from a study conducted by my advisee, Jason Grebe, in order to complete his master's degree in the Communication Studies Department at the University of Kansas in the spring of 2009. Participants were 120 undergraduate students at KU. Sixty males and 60 females participated, and participants had an average age of 20. Seventy-five participants (62 percent) were single and 45 were in a relationship (38 percent). After completing the Flirting Styles Inventory and other prestudy measures on an online survey, study participants interacted in cross-sex dyads using Instant Messenger. After interacting for 20 minutes, they completed a postinteraction survey about how much they liked and perceived liking from their partner. The results of Jason Grebe's thesis, which did not include analysis of the flirting styles data, can be found in "Affinity in Instant Messaging," published in the spring 2013 issue of *Northwest Journal of Communication*.

The final sample was drawn from a new survey linked to the online Flirting Styles Inventory that had questions that were different from the first three study samples. This survey was available from November 1, 2011 through June 1, 2012, and 400 respondents were retained in the final sample. As in the FSI Survey, respondents were retained when they completed three study measures, including the FSI, and did not show evidence of faked data based on age and gender questions.

The Flirting Styles Inventory was developed in consultation with research on heterosexual romantic relationships. The claims in this book are only applicable to heterosexual individuals, since anyone who responded to my survey and was self-reported to be gay, lesbian, bisexual or transgender was not included in the reported analysis. Although I enthusiastically look forward to finding out if the five styles also apply to gay and lesbian relationships, that remains a topic of future research, for now.

ANALYSES

All the claims regarding the five flirting styles and not attributed to other published research originated from one of these four samples. The majority of the claims reported in this book were made from analyses using Ordinary Least Squares regression. All claims regarding the effect of any given flirting style on some outcome variable were controlled for all other flirting styles as well as respondent age, gender and relationship status (single versus seriously dating or more). This means that if a Sincere flirting style was related to some behavior or attitude, this relationship was not due to the influence of any other of the four flirting styles or the respondents' age, gender or relationship status.

Furthermore, the first two samples were large and prone to committing Type 1 error (i.e., claiming a relationship is significant when it is actually due to chance). Therefore, claims in this book regarding the relationship between any given flirting style and some dating or attitudinal variable are significant at $p < .001$ and change in R-squared $> .01$. That is, all relationships reported in this book were statistically significant beyond chance levels, explained over 1 percent of the variance in the outcome variable and were not due to variation that could be attributed to any other flirting style or the respondents' age, gender or relationship status. Gender-specific relationships (i.e., "men believe that...") were found using the same criteria as above after splitting the file by respondent gender. Finally, whenever I make the claim, "This is the only style related to X," it means that only that particular flirting style significantly predicted X.

In cases where I claim, "This flirting style is X percent more likely to..." I used logistic regression because that particular outcome variable was dichotomous. For example, respondents were allowed to pick only one option in response to the question, "Where did you meet your last relationship partner?" All responses were treated as dummy codes (e.g., 1 = work, 0 = some other location) in logistic regression. The most accurate wording of that type of claim is, "Compared with people low on this flirting style, people high on this flirting style were X percent more likely to meet at X location compared with any other place they might have met."

Claims drawn from the fourth sample were also made using OLS regression. Probability values were still set at $p < .001$, but the R-square change requirement was relaxed due to the smaller sample size.

Claims drawn from the interaction data from Jason Grebe's thesis project appear primarily in the "Cyber-flirting" boxes. In these claims, regression was not used because the sample was small and many claims were gender-specific (i.e., only applying to women or men). All reported relationships are taken from bivariate correlations between each flirting style and study outcomes.

ENDNOTES

Chapter One: The Five Flirting Styles

For years, school, work, and through friends (box)...Finkel, E. J., Eastwick, P. W. Karney, B. R., Reis, H. T., & Sprecher, S. (in press). Online dating: A critical analysis from the perspective of psychological science. *Psychological Science.*

After years of slow, steady growth...Sprecher, S., Schwartz, P., Harvey, J., & Hatfield, E. (2008). TheBusinessofLove.com: Relationship initiation at internet matchmaking services. In S. Sprecher, A. Wenzel, & J. Harvey (Eds.), *Handbook of relationship initiation* (pp. 249-268). New York: Psychology Press, Taylor and Francis Group.

In addition to the well-known...La France, B. H., Henningsen, D. D., Oates, A., & Shaw, C. M. (2009). Social-sexual interactions? Meta-analyses of sex differences in perceptions of flirtatiousness, seductiveness, and promiscuousness. *Communication Monographs, 76,* 263-285.

One study concluded that flirting...Farris, C., Treat, T. A., Viken, R. J., & McFall, R. M. (2008). Perceptual mechanisms that characterize gender differences in decoding women's sexual intent. *Psychological Science, 19,* 348-354.

Another challenge in figuring out...Henningsen, D. D. (2004). Flirting with meaning: An examination of miscommunication in flirting interactions. *Sex Roles, 50,* 481-489.

Elizabeth Paul and her colleagues found that...Paul, E. L., McManus, B., & Hayes, A. (2000). "Hookups": Characteristics and correlates of college students' spontaneous and anonymous sexual experiences. *The Journal of Sex Research, 37*, 76-88.

In one study of young adults . . . Furman, W., & Shaffer, L. (2011). Romantic partners, friends, friends with benefits, and casual acquaintances as sexual partners. *Journal of Sex Research, 48*, 554-564.

Dick Barelds and Pieternel Barelds-Dijkstra, a pair of . . . Barelds, D.P.H., & Barelds-Dijkstra, P. (2007). Love at first sight or friends first? Ties among partner personality trait similarity, relationship onset, relationship quality, and love. *Journal of Social and Personal Relationships, 24*, 479-496.

Although this was less common than . . . Barelds & Barelds-Dijkstra, 2007.

When people go on dates, the . . . Mongeau, P. A., Serewicz, M.C.M., & Therrien, L. F. (2004). Goals for cross-sex first dates: Identification, measurement, and the influence of contextual factors. *Communication Monographs, 71*, 121-147.

Barelds and Barelds-Dijkstra estimate that about . . . Barelds & Barelds-Dijkstra, 2007.

No matter what your pathway to (box) . . . Barelds & Barelds-Dijkstra, 2007.

Seeking an emotional connection with a . . . Clark, C. L., Shaver, P. R., & Abrahams, M. F. (1999). Strategic behaviors in romantic relationship initiation. *Personality and Social Psychology Bulletin, 25*, 709-722.

Men are the aggressors and women . . . La France, B. H. (2010). What verbal and nonverbal communication cues lead to sex? An analysis of the traditional sexual script. *Communication Quarterly, 58*, 297-318.

Chapter Two: The Physical Style

Dr. Monica Moore, a pioneering researcher in . . . Moore, M. M. (1985). Nonverbal courtship patterns in women: Context and consequences. *Ethology & Sociobiology, 6*, 237-247.

In the 1950s, famous social scientist (box) . . . Coontz, S. (2005). *Marriage, a history.* New York: Penguin.

One study found that when there are women . . . Renninger, L. A., Wade, T. J., & Grammer, K. (2004). Getting that female glance: patterns and consequences of male nonverbal behavior in courtship contexts. *Evolution and Human Behavior, 25*, 416-431.

Men take a more dominant role . . . La France, 2010; McDaniel, A. K. (2005). Young women's dating behavior: Why/why not date a nice guy? *Sex Roles, 53*, 347-359.

But women often take a leading . . . Moore, M. M. (2010). Human nonverbal courtship behavior: A brief historical review. *Journal of Sex Research, 47*, 171-180.

It is pretty obvious that women . . . Schmitt, D. P. (2002). A meta-analysis of sex differences in romantic attraction: Do rating contexts affect tactic effectiveness judgments? *British Journal of Social Psychology, 41*, 387-402.

Going out to party and hooking . . . Paul, E. L. (2006). Beer goggles, catching feelings, and the walk of shame: The myths and realities of the hookup experience.

In D. C. Kirkpatrick, S. Duck, & M. K. Foley (Eds.), *Relating difficulty: The process of constructing and managing difficult interaction* (pp. 141-160). Mahwah, NJ: Erlbaum.

While there isn't a lot of...Moore, 2010.

Young men report using mock aggression (box)...Ballard, M. E., Green, S., & Granger, C. (2003). Affiliation, flirting, and fun: Mock aggressive behavior in college students. *Psychological Record, 53,* 33-49.

Physical Flirts will send more messages (box)...Grebe, J. P., & Hall, J. A. (2013). Affinity in instant messaging. *Northwest Journal of Communication.*

Some time ago, Dr. Linda Koeppel and her...Koeppel, L. B., Montagne-Miller, Y., O'Hair, D., & Cody, M. J. (1993). Friendly? Flirting? Wrong? In P. J. Kalbfleisch (Ed.), *Interpersonal communication: Evolving interpersonal relationships* (pp. 13-32). Hillsdale, NJ: Erlbaum.

When chatting online, Physical flirts think (box)...Grebe & Hall, 2013.

Some recent research by a pair of...Penke, L., & Asendorpf, J. B. (2008). Beyond global sociosexual orientations: A more differentiated look at sociosexuality and its effects on courtship and romantic relationships. *Journal of Personality and Social Psychology, 95,* 1113-1135.

The most common reason for engaging (box)...Weaver, S. J. & Harold, E. S. (2000). Casual sex and women: Measurement and motivational issues. *Journal of Psychology & Human Sexuality, 12,* 23-41.

There is good reason to believe...Penke & Asendorpf, 2008.

As one researcher put it...McDaniel, 2005.

Don't try to convert a guy into (box)...Meston, C. M., & Buss, D. M. (2009). *Why women have sex.* New York: Henry Holt & Co.

The Love Attitudes scale was created...Hendrick, C., Hendrick, S., & Dicke, A. (1998). The love attitudes scale: Short form. *Journal of Social and Personal Relationships, 15,* 147-159.

We know that people with a...Paul, McManus, & Hayes, 2000.

Chapter Three: The Polite Style

Men are more likely than women...La France et al., 2009.

These things may inspire women...Koeppel et al., 1993.

In addition, if women are too...Koeppel et al., 1993.

Individuals aged 40 and over have...Coontz, 2005.

There is also the issue of...Ballard et al., 2003.

Because they were once the focus...Coontz, 2005.

This makes sense, given the fact...Baker, L. R., & Oswald, D. L. (2010). Shyness and online social networking services. *Journal of Social and Personal Relationships, 27,* 873-889.

Because of the way they fall in love (box)...Paul, McManus, & Hayes, 2000.

Although people think that there is (box)...Furman & Shaffer, 2011.

Love born in friendship . . . Morrow, G. D., Clark, E. M., & Brock, K. F. (1995). Individual and partner love styles: Implications for the quality of romantic involvements. *Journal of Social and Personal Relationships, 12,* 363-387.

Chapter Four: The Playful Style

Men and women are equally motivated to flirt (box) . . . Henningsen, 2004.

People that age believe there is . . . Arnett, J. J. (2004). *Emerging adulthood.* New York: Oxford University Press.

Because she thinks you like her and (box) . . . Grebe & Hall, 2013.

Research tells us that there are . . . Hendrick, C., & Hendrick, S. (1986). A theory and method of love. *Journal of Personality and Social Psychology, 50,* 392-402.

In an extensive study of hooking . . . Paul, McManus, & Hayes, 2000.

Once in a relationship, people tend to stop (box) . . . Paul, McManus, & Hayes, 2000.

Women who like to date Playful and flirty guys (box) . . . McDaniel, 2005.

Chapter Five: The Sincere Style

The Sincere Flirt knows that . . . Clark, R. A., Dockum, M., Hazeu, H., Huang, M., Luo, N., Ramsey, J., & Spyrou, A. (2004). Initial encounters of young men and women: Impressions and disclosure estimates. *Sex Roles, 50,* 699-710; Hess, J. A., Fannin, A. D., & Pollom, L. H. (2007). Creating closeness: Discerning and measuring strategies for fostering closer relationships. *Personal Relationships, 14,* 25-44.

When you share information about yourself (box) . . . Clark et al., 2004.

Women tend to like men who . . . Cunningham, M. R. (1989). Reactions to heterosexual opening gambits: Female selectivity and male responsiveness. *Personality and Social Psychology Bulletin, 15,* 27-41; Kleinke, C. L., Meeker, F. B., & Staneski, R. A. (1986). Preference for opening lines: Comparing ratings by men and women. *Sex Roles, 15,* 585-600.

Past research has shown that emotional . . . Clark et al., 1999.

According to studies using brain-scanning (box) . . . Meston & Buss, 2009.

In a study I did on online . . . Hall, J. A., Park, N., Song, H., & Cody, M. J. (2010). Strategic misrepresentation in online dating: The effects of gender, self-monitoring, and personality traits. *Journal of Social and Personal Relationships, 27,* 117-135.

We all know that the nice . . . Regan, P. C., Levin, L., Sprecher, S., Christopher, F. S., & Cate, R. (2000). Partner preferences: What characteristics do men and women desire in their short-term sexual and long-term romantic partners? *Journal of Psychology & Human Sexuality, 12,* 1-18.

(Although there are internet dating sites . . . Finkel et al., in press.

The first date is the leap . . . Mongeau et al., 2004.

You probably don't need research on . . . Mongeau et al., 2004.

The very fact that they decided...Morr, M. C., & Mongeau, P. A. (2004). First-date expectations: The impact of sex of initiator, alcohol consumption, and relationship type. *Communication Research, 31,* 3-35.

Communication theorist Kelly Albada...Albada, K. F., Knapp, M. L., & Theune, K. E. (2002). Interaction appearance theory: Changing perceptions of physical attractiveness through social interaction. *Communication Theory, 12,* 8-40.

"He always had something to say"...Albada et al., 2002, p. 21.

A follow-up study conducted by three different...Lewandowski, G. W., Aron, A., & Gee, J. (2007). Personality goes a long way: The malleability of opposite-sex physical attractiveness. *Personal Relationships, 14,* 571-585.

A man's physical attractiveness is more (box)...Lewandowski, Aron, & Gee, 2007.

Showing warmth, openness and emotional involvement (box)...Sanderson, C. A. (2004). The link between the pursuit of intimacy goals and satisfaction in close relationships: An examination of the underlying processes. In D. J. Mashek & A. P. Aron (Eds.), *Handbook of closeness and intimacy* (pp. 247-266). Mahwah, NJ: Erlbaum.

Several studies have explored the "nice guy"...McDaniel, 2005; Urbaniak, G. C., & Kilmann, P. R. (2003). Physical attractiveness and the "nice guy paradox": Do nice guys really finish last? *Sex Roles, 49,* 413-426; Urbaniak, G. C., & Kilmann, P. R. (2006). Niceness and dating success: A further test of the nice guy stereotype. *Sex Roles, 55,* 209-224.

In fact, jerks are exemplified by...Urbaniak & Kilmann, 2006.

You can tell if a guy is a jerk (box)...Bale, C., Morrison, R., & Caryl, P. G. (2006). Chat-up lines as male sexual displays. *Personality and Individual Differences, 40,* 655-664.

Both men and women have sex (box)...Meston & Buss, 2009.

Specifically, men are expected to take...La France, 2010.

They generally seek out love...Hendrick et al., 1998.

A social psychology researcher named...Sanderson, C. A., & Cantor, N. (1995). Social dating goals in late adolescence: Implications for safe sexual activity. *Journal of Personality and Social Psychology, 68,* 1121-1134.; Sanderson, C. A., Keiter, E. J., Miles, M. G., & Yopyk, D.J.A. (2007). The association between intimacy goals and plans for initiating dating relationships. *Personal Relationships, 14,* 225-243.

Men and women are equally likely to (box)...Sanderson et al., 2007.

The more comfortable you feel talking (box)...Clark et al., 2004.

Chapter Six: The Traditional Style

Men who have a stereotypically masculine personality (box)...Clark et al., 1999.

Men think that women who initiate...Koeppel et al., 1993.

However, whether men (or women) like...Coontz, 2005.

People know that, traditionally, it is...La France, 2010.

People believe this to be true . . . de Weerth, C., & Kalma, A. (1995). Gender differences in awareness of courtship initiation tactics. *Sex Roles, 32,* 717-734.

A woman who is a little . . . Koeppel et al., 1993.

In the early 1900s, women invited (box) . . . Coontz, 2005.

Until the arrival of the automobile . . . Coontz, 2005.

When *dating* (the term was new . . . Coontz, 2005.

Without question, there are real risks . . . Paul, 2006.

Using Instant Messenger to flirt leaves (box) . . . Grebe & Hall, 2013.

When a society is more traditional . . . Glick, P., & Fiske, S. T. (2001). An ambivalent alliance: Hostile and benevolent sexism as complementary justifications for gender inequality. *American Psychologist, 56,* 109-118.

In more traditional cultures, heroic men . . . Rudman, L. A., & Heppen, J. (2003). Implicit romantic fantasies and women's interest in personal power: A glass slipper effect? *Personality and Social Psychology Bulletin, 29,* 1357-1370.

There is good evidence that, when . . . Schmitt, D. P. (2005). Fundamentals of human mating strategies. In D. M. Buss (Ed.), *The evolutionary psychology handbook* (pp. 258-291). New York: Wiley.

For the Traditional flirt, however, this . . . Travaglia, L. K., Overall, N. C., & Sibley, C. G. (2009). Benevolent and hostile sexism and preferences for romantic partners. *Personality and Individual Differences, 47,* 599-604.

Similarly, the Traditional woman may be . . . Johannesen-Schmidt, M. C., & Eagly, A. H. (2002). Another look at sex differences in preferred mate characteristics: The effects of endorsing the traditional female gender role. *Psychology of Women Quarterly, 26,* 322-328.

In the late 1950s, two-thirds (box) . . . Coontz, 2005.

In fact, if a woman is . . . Fowers, A. F., & Fowers, B. J. (2010). Social dominance and sexual self-schema as moderators of sexist reactions to female subtypes. *Sex Roles, 62,* 468-480.

For women, particularly, agreeing to these . . . Viki, G. T., Abrams, D., & Hutchison, P. (2003). The "true" romantic: Benevolent sexism and paternalistic chivalry. *Sex Roles, 49,* 533-537.

Women, but not men, think that (box) . . . Clark et al., 1999.

Because a Traditional lady isn't putting . . . Penke & Asendorpf, 2008.

When Traditional men communicate with women (box) . . . Grebe & Hall, 2013.

In my research with Melanie Canterberry . . . Hall, J. A., & Canterberry, M. (2011). Sexism and assertive courtship strategies. *Sex Roles, 65,* 840-854.

Chapter Seven: The Switch

Physical flirts can get real personal (box) . . . Grebe & Hall, 2013.

Researchers of human sexuality typically identify . . . Meston & Buss, 2009, p. 144.

Research says: This simply isn't . . . Fisher, T. D., Moore, Z. T., & Pittenger, M. J. (2012).

Sex on the brain?: An examination of frequency of sexual cognitions as a function of gender, erotophilia, and social desirability. *Journal of Sex Research, 49*, 69-77.

Being in a relationship heavily dampens . . . Penke & Asendorpf, 2008.

People who are in relationships, especially . . . Bleske-Rechek, A. E., Somers, E., Micke, C., et al. (2012). Benefit or burden? Attraction in cross-sex friendship. *Journal of Social and Personal Relationships, 29*, 569-596.

When people are in unhappy relationships (box) . . . O'Farrell, K. J., Rosenthal, E. V., & O'Neal, E. C. (2003). Relationship satisfaction and responsiveness to nonmates' flirtation: Testing an evolutionary explanation. *Journal of Social and Personal Relationships, 20*, 663-674.

Crucially, when we are in a . . . Bredow, C. A., Cate, R., & Huston, T. (2008). Have we met before? A conceptual model of first romantic encounters. In S. Sprecher, A. Wenzel, & J. Harvey (Eds.), *Handbook of relationship initiation* (pp. 3-28). New York: Psychology Press.

Easily one of the top-rated . . . Sprecher, S., & Felmlee, D. (2008). Insider perspectives on attraction. In Sprecher, Wenzel, & Harvey (Eds.), *Handbook of relationship initiation* (pp. 297-314).

The discovery of *mutual* attraction makes . . . Sprecher, S. (1998). Insiders' perspectives on reasons for attraction to a close other. *Social Psychology Quarterly, 61*, 287-300.

You start feeling better and better . . . Bredow, Cate, & Huston, 2008.

They don't want to put pressure . . . Kunkel, A. D., Wilson, S. R., Olufowote, J., & Robson, S. (2003). Identifying implications of influence goals: Initiating, intensifying, and ending romantic relationships. *Western Journal of Communication, 67*, 382-412.

Women don't know they are signaling . . . de Weerth & Kalma, 1995.

One of the most exciting sexual . . . Renaud, C. A. & Byers, E. S. (1999). Exploring the frequency, diversity, and content of university students' positive and negative sexual cognitions. *The Canadian Journal of Human Sexuality, 8*, 17-30.

A recent study on women who . . . MacGregor, J.C.D., & Cavallo, J. V. (2011). Breaking the rules: Personal control increases women's direct relationship initiation. *Journal of Social and Personal Relationships, 28*, 848-867.

A lot of hookups occur under . . . Paul, E. L., Wenzel, A., & Harvey, J. (2008). Hookups: A facilitator or a barrier to relationship initiation and intimacy development? In Sprecher, Wenzel, Harvey (Eds.), *Handbook of relationship initiation* (pp. 375-390).

People who seek attention above all . . . Penke & Asendorpf, 2008.

Chapter Eight: Perceptions and Misperceptions

Consider this research study: when people . . . Fichten, C. S., Tagalakis, V., Judd, D., Wright, J., & Amsel, R. (1992). Verbal and nonverbal communication cues in daily conversation and dating. *Journal of Social Psychology, 132*, 751-769.

A recent exciting study by Dr. Coreen Farris...Farris et al., 2008.

In one of the most advanced...Grammer, K., Kruck, K., Juette, A., & Fink, B. (2000). Non-verbal behavior as courtship signals: The role of control and choice in selecting partners. *Evolution and Human Behavior, 21,* 371-390.

In fact, when the most transparent...Place, S. S., Todd, P. M., & Asendorpf, J. B. (2009). The ability to judge the romantic interest of others. *Psychological Science, 20,* 22-26.

Twenty-six percent of women have had (box)...Farris et al., 2008.

One of the most consistent findings...La France et al., 2009.

The theory is that it would...Haselton, M. G., & Buss, D. M. (2000). Error management theory: A new perspective on biases in cross-sex mind reading. *Journal of Personality and Social Psychology, 78,* 81-91.

The third possibility is that men...McClure, E. B. (2000). A meta-analytic review of sex differences in facial expression processing and their development in infants, children, and adolescents. *Psychological Bulletin, 126,* 424-453.

If someone is obviously flirting with (box)...Clark et al., 1999.

A man perceives each of these four...Moore, M. M. (2002). Courtship communication and perception. *Perceptual and Motor Skills, 94,* 97-105.

Women know that women do it...de Weerth & Kalma, 1995.

Although attractive women are approached more...Moore, 1985.

While women tend to do this...Renninger et al., 2004.

For example, a woman could pretend...Moore, 1985.

As a downside, guys who lean...Simpson, J. A., Gangestad, S. W., & Biek, M. (1993). Personality and nonverbal social behavior: An ethological perspective of relationship initiation. *Journal of Experimental Social Psychology, 29,* 434-461.

People who smile more are more...Houser, M. L., Horan, S. M., & Furler, L. A. (2008). Dating in the fast lane: How communication predicts speed-dating success. *Journal of Social and Personal Relationships, 25,* 749-768.

People who are more engaged also...Houser et al., 2008.

When a woman talks with her hands...Grammer et al., 2000.

But, more than anything, guys laugh...Simpson et al., 1993.

And if a guy can get...Penke & Asendorpf, 2008.

The more time that people spend...Penke & Asendorpf, 2008.

Indeed, if a woman is dressed...Grammer, K., Renninger, L., & Fischer, B. (2004). Disco clothing, female sexual motivation, and relationship status: Is she dressed to impress? *Journal of Sex Research, 41,* 66-74.

But if she *is* single, then...Grammer et al., 2004.

Men can more accurately distinguish sexually (box)...Farris et al., 2008.

A flirt may be trying to...Henningsen, 2004; Koeppel et al., 1993.

Because some people are able to...Grammer et al., 2000; Simpson et al., 1993.

Consider the fact that some of...Grammer et al., 2000.

A classic study on pickup lines...Kleinke et al., 1986.

Instead, lines that are sweet and...Senko, C., & Fyffe, V. (2010). An evolutionary perspective on effective vs. ineffective pick-up lines. *The Journal of Social Psychology, 150*, 648–667.

When chatting up somebody, you've got (box)...Grammer et al., 2000.

The two clearest negative signals a...Grammer et al., 2000.

People who are already in a...Place et al., 2009.

Chapter Nine: Common Mistakes and Helpful Hints

Hookups at the bar only end...Paul et al., 2008.

One of the best ways to...Weber, K., Goodboy, A. K., & Cayanus, J. L. (2010). Flirting competence: An experimental study on appropriate and effective opening lines. *Communication Research Reports, 27*, 184–191.

For some people, attraction just (box)...Derlega, V. J., Winstead, B. A., & Green, K. (2008). Self-disclosure and starting a close relationship. In Sprecher, Wenzel, & Harvey (Eds.), *Handbook of relationship initiation* (pp. 153–174).

Guys who sit with an open...Renninger et al., 2004.

Becoming more comfortable with flirting takes (box)...Berger, C. R., & Bell, R. A. (1988). Plan and the initiation of social relationships. *Human Communication Research, 15*, 217–235.

In fact, a guy talking too...Grammer et al., 2000.

Displaying a good sense of humor...Meston & Buss, 2009, p. 21.

According to speed-dating studies, women (box)...Kurzban, R., & Weeden, J. (2005). HurryDate: Mate preferences in action. *Evolution and Human Behavior, 26*, 227–244.

If you know your crush's friends...Sprecher, S. (2011). The influence of social networks on romantic relationships: Through the lens of the social network. *Personal Relationships, 18*, 630–644.

ACKNOWLEDGMENTS

The contents of this book are drawn from years of work made possible by opportunities that others have given me, the time and energy of collaborators and friends, and the never-ending support of my family.

I would like to start by thanking the over 10,000 people who completed either the eHarmony or the Flirting Styles Inventory Survey. Without their willingness to share their attitudes, opinions and experiences, I would not have been able to write this book. My special thanks to the 22 individuals who agreed to do in-depth interviews about dating and flirting with me or my research assistant, Leah Sheahan. Although their names and ages have been changed, their real-world stories provided me exceptional insights that I am able to share with you.

I would like to thank my advisor, Michael Cody, and Steve Carter from eHarmony. Without the vast network of connections that Cody has built over the years, including our key intermediary, Julie Albright, I would have never met Steve. Cody also deserves thanks for introducing me to several essential readings in flirting and courtship, including his own research. Steve's support over the years has been outstanding. Although very busy, Steve has always made time to respond to my emails about the *Communication Quarterly* publication, this book, and the data gathered from eHarmony's volunteers. I would also like to thank Sheila Murphy and the Annenberg School of Communication for research support in the early days of designing the Flirting Styles Inventory.

I would like to thank Jill Jess and the Media Relations team at the University of Kansas, whose interest in my work made the initial press release and the online FSI a reality. Beth Innocenti, my former department chair, has been nothing less than an enthusiastic and energetic proponent of my work, and I thank her for it. There are several undergraduate research collaborators I would like to thank, including Leah Sheahan, Robin Latham and Courtney Holle. Each brought energy and personal insight to my work. My thanks to Jason Grebe for letting me include the FSI as part of his cool project on impression formation on Instant Messenger, and to my graduate advisee Natalie Pennington for reading a draft of the book.

I would like to thank my agent, Linda Konner, for believing in this project and artfully guiding it through the selection of a publisher. Linda played a key role in helping me learn the ins and outs of attracting a publisher and has been a stalwart supporter of this book from the beginning. I would like to thank my friend Roly Allen for his help in fashioning a proposal and query letter prior to meeting Linda.

I would also thank my editor, Sarah Pelz, and the team at Harlequin Nonfiction. Sarah has been a patient and enthusiastic supporter of my work. I printed out the email she sent me after reading the first few chapters because it contained so much excitement that it infused me with the energy to keep writing.

I have a terrific family who deserves thanks for so very many things above and beyond their support of this book. For now, I want to give thanks for my parents, Maura and Steve, who were both proud and thrilled about this project from the very beginning. Despite the length of the process, they couldn't wait to ask me how the book was going at every single turn. They are my biggest cheerleaders and two sources of endless support. I would like to thank my brothers, Nathan and Eric, for their interest and support.

Several close friends deserve special thanks. I would like to thank Brad Douglass, Craig Hammill and Bambi Logue for reading early drafts of this book, providing me helpful encouragement about the process and sharing in the excitement of it all. My thanks to Melanie Canterberry for reading the book closely and carefully, and for being a great collaborator on our sexism and *The Game* project. My thanks go to Marcia Dawkins, a champion for my cause, a dear friend, and a model of fearlessness. I would also like to thank my web designer Harry Guillermo and logo designer Austin Griffis.

I offer my dearest and most sincere thanks to my wife, Amber. Her support and confidence in me have been essential

at every step of this process, from managing the media attention and gaining confidence to pitching the book back in 2010 to
enduring the months of work writing and rewriting chapters, and
through seeing the work to completion. I could not ask for a better partner in life. Thanks for picking up on my flirting style. And
my thanks to my little boy, Graham, for infusing my life with joy.

INDEX